# WHERE JESUS WALKED

# WHERE JESUS WALKED

## THE LAND AND CULTURE OF
## NEW TESTAMENT TIMES

D. KELLY OGDEN

Deseret Book Company
Salt Lake City, Utah

Photographs on cover, pages 61 (top left and right, center left and right), and 70 (center left) courtesy of Richard Cleave. Photograph on page 70 (bottom left) courtesy of Lamar C. Berrett. Photographs on pages 54 (bottom right) and 80 (top right) courtesy of Dan Noorlander. Photograph on page 131 (top right) courtesy of Tim Taggart. Photographs on pages 35 (top left), 80 (bottom right), and 131 (center left) and maps 1 and 5 courtesy of the Church Educational System, © The Church of Jesus Christ of Latter-day Saints. Used by permission. All other photographs and maps are the author's.

**Library of Congress Cataloging-in-Publication Data**

Ogden, D. Kelly (Daniel Kelly), 1947–
   Where Jesus walked : the land and culture of New Testament times / D. Kelly Ogden.
      p.   cm.
   Includes bibliographical references and indexes.
   ISBN 0-87579-530-7
   1. Palestine—Historical geography.   2. Jews—Civilization—To 70 A.D.   3. Bible. N.T.—Geography.   4. Jesus Christ—Parables. I. Title.
DS108.9.O35   1991
225.9'1—dc20                                                    91-11411
                                                                    CIP

Printed in Mexico

10   9   8   7   6   5   4   3   2   1

# CONTENTS

v

# LIST OF MAPS

# ACKNOWLEDGMENTS

The initial encouragement for writing this book came from Professor Menashe Har-El of Tel Aviv University, who is a renowned biblical geographer in the state of Israel.

The following also deserve expression of gratitude in print:

My former research assistant, Daniel B. Galbraith, for his remarkable research and organizational skills, which helped give reality to this work from its inception.

Several seminary and institute teachers and Brigham Young University religion faculty, who read the first draft of the manuscript and offered suggestions, and especially Dr. Richard Lloyd Anderson, professor of ancient scripture and history at BYU, for his careful examination of the text and helpful recommendations.

Richard Tice and Kent Ware of Deseret Book, who guided this volume through its final stages from editing to publication.

I thank other faculty members and many students who joined me during a fourteen-year span of time (1976–90) in literally walking *where Jesus walked*. Over the years, we walked the ninety-two miles with Joseph and Mary from Nazareth to Bethlehem, and we followed in the footsteps of Jesus from Jerusalem to Jericho, from the Sea of Galilee to Caesarea Philippi, from Nazareth and Cana to the Sea of Galilee, from Chorazin and from Bethsaida to Capernaum, from Galilee one hundred miles south to Jerusalem, and on many other walks. Thousands of young Latter-day Saints have now had opportunity to study the life and teachings of Jesus around the Sea of Galilee and the events of the last week of Jesus' life, the greatest week in history, in Jerusalem.

Special thanks to two dear friends. The first, Dr. Ellis T. Rasmussen, former dean of Religious Education at BYU, with whom I worked for years on the new editions of the scriptures, and who during that time encouraged me to pursue the biblical studies that he could see I loved. Perhaps to him I owe the fact that one of my favorite words in the English language is *biblical*. The second friend, to whom I attribute many of the sweetest memories of my teaching career, is Dr. David B. Galbraith, for two decades a guiding light in our work in Jerusalem and the founding director of the Jerusalem Center for Near Eastern Studies.

Finally, I acknowledge deepest gratitude to my faithful companion, Marcia Hammond Ogden, who endured all those years in a faraway land, in sometimes spartan conditions, so that I could walk where Jesus walked and teach where Jesus taught. She has been my nearest example of living how Jesus lived.

And our children—most of whom were born in Jerusalem and baptized in the Jordan River—may they never forget the land of their nativity and always remember not only the value of walking where Jesus walked, but also the importance of walking *as* Jesus walked.

Dr. D. Kelly Ogden
Brigham Young University
Spring 1991

# INTRODUCTION

Jesus of Nazareth was a master teacher. As did all the great Hebrew poets and prophets before him, Jesus consistently drew from his geographical milieu to illustrate his teachings. A favorite oratorical and literary technique in Jesus' day was to demonstrate how something in nature was comparable to something in the human experience.

The more people become acquainted with the land of Jesus, the more they will understand the imagery and symbols drawn from the Holy Land. Goethe once said, *"Wer den Dichter will verstehen muss in Dichter's Lande gehen"* ("Whoever would understand a poet must go to the poet's homeland").

After Nephi wrote that his soul delighted in the words of Isaiah and that he understood them, he explained why: "I came out from Jerusalem, and mine eyes hath beheld the things of the Jews, and I know that . . . there is none other people that understand the things which were spoken unto the Jews like unto them, save it be that they are taught after the manner of the things of the Jews. . . . Behold, I, of myself, have dwelt at Jerusalem, wherefore I know concerning *the regions round about.*" (2 Ne. 25:5–6; italics added.) Nephi could understand and appreciate Isaiah because of his personal knowledge of Isaiah's environment.

Elder Orson Hyde learned the value of knowing something about the land of the Bible in his visit there a century and a half ago: "Almost everything which the traveller beholds is a standing illustration of some portion of scripture: for example, I saw two women grinding wheat at a little hand-mill, consisting of two small stones with a little rude tackling about it, the whole of which one man might take in his arms and carry almost any where at pleasure. One would turn the top stone until her strength was exhausted, and then the other would take her place, and so alternately keep the little grinder in operation. It appears that our Lord foresaw the perpetuity of this custom, even to the time of his second coming; for he said, 'Two women shall be grinding at the mill; one shall be taken and the other left'; and for aught I know, these two I saw were the identical ones. I also saw the people take a kind of coarse grass and mix it with some kind of earth or peat that had been wet and reduced to the consistency of common mortar, and then lay it out in flattened cakes to dry for fuel. I then, for the first time in my life, saw the propriety of our Savior's allusion, 'If God so clothe the grass of the field, which to-day is, and to-morrow is cast into the oven, &c.' "[1]

A more recent testimonial confirms Elder Hyde's conclusion—there is great value in knowing something about the land in which Jesus taught: " 'All things bear record of me.' (Moses 6:63.) So we have been taught. But when our feet first touched the ground of Israel more than a decade ago, we still cherished the fallacy that the Master's words were the only vehicle for his gospel message. Environment and circumstance mattered little if at all, we thought. We soon learned otherwise! During his ministry, the Teacher of teachers invoked his surroundings to verify his revelatory acts and sayings. The cosmos was his visual aid, and the setting sprang to life through his words and actions. In the very rocks, in the very fountains and mountains, in the very trees of Israel his meaning is lodged—meanings that can reach the center of the soul."[2]

The words of Jesus are richly replete with images reflecting the agricultural and pastoral background of his countrymen. He used highly picturesque figures of speech from the contemporary world of fauna and flora, from the land, from phenomena of nature, and from climate, rainfall, and other meteorological conditions.

*Where Jesus Walked: The Land and Culture of New Testament Times* is an attempt to identify all things geographical in the teachings of Jesus and the early apostles and to elucidate not only their surface meaning but also their deep meaning—how some object or condition in the land of Jesus is comparable to human conduct or character. The land of the Bible has been immortalized through the universal lessons that were drawn from it. To be sure, the masterful messages cannot be fully understood without some knowledge of their physical settings.

The general subject of each chapter is divided into various appropriate topics. Each topic is entitled and introduced by a specific passage of scripture that relates directly to that topic.

The King James Version of the Bible is used in the text because it is still the single most popular version in use worldwide and because of its superior literary quality. The King James Version admirably preserves the style and tone and reverence of the biblical expression. Unlike many modern versions that seek to expunge all provincial and cultural idioms and figures—which are often the key to understanding analogies made by the Jewish writers—the King James Version in most cases eloquently captures the sense and meaning of the ancient text.

The reader is now invited to examine anew the virtue of the word of God by exploring the physical settings of the revelations, hopefully uncovering some heretofore hidden treasures of knowledge.

NOTES

1. Orson Hyde, *A Voice from Jerusalem, or A Sketch of the Travels and Ministry of Elder Orson Hyde* (Boston: Albert Morgan, 1842), 18.

2. Truman G. Madsen, "The Olive Press," *Ensign,* December 1982, p. 57.

# GEOGRAPHY, LANDSCAPES, AND ROADS

*"They shall come from the east, and from the west, and from the north, and from the south." (Luke 13:29.)*

The word *orient* means east. The most important direction for the ancient inhabitant of the Holy Land was east, and all directions are given in the Bible as if standing looking east. Abraham and his servants pursued their enemies "unto Hobah, which is on the left hand [that is, north] of Damascus." (Gen. 14:15.) Isaiah 9:12 records a warning that enemies are ready to devour Israel, the Syrians "before" and the Philistines "behind," meaning east and west.

Most Semitic peoples, who included the Hebrews, regarded east, where the sun rose, with directional priority, though the ancient Egyptians viewed south-north as the paramount axis, since the Nile was their source of life. Because water was plentiful and constant and because the sun represented the other essential element of life, the Egyptians generally held the sun as chief god.

It is something of a paradox, then, that inhabitants of eastern Mediterranean countries (the Levant), who lived in desert lands and depended so much on the rains, would not attach the greatest significance to the west, whence came the rains. They did worship Baal and Hadad and others who were storm gods, and there were gods of the sea, yet priority is given to the east. Temporal salvation, the waters of life, may come from the west—"When ye see a cloud rise out of the west, straightway ye say, There cometh a shower; and so it is" (Luke 12:54)—but spiritual salvation would come from the east—"For as the lightning cometh out of the east . . . so shall also the coming of the Son of man be" (Matt. 24:27).

Alfred Edersheim, an authority on Jewish tradition, wrote, "The star shall shine forth from the East, and this is the star of the Messiah."[1] "There came wise men from the east to Jerusalem," having seen "his star in the east" at Jesus' birth. (Matt. 2:1–2.) Making his final and triumphal entry into the Holy City, Jesus commenced his journey from Bethphage, a village at the easternmost limit of the city at that time.

Isaiah foresaw the coming of the Messiah in the end of days and he asked, "Who is this that cometh from Edom [that is, from the east] . . . glorious in his ap-

3

parel, travelling in the greatness of his strength?" And the answer: "I that speak in righteousness, mighty to save." (Isa. 63:1.)

*"But they, supposing him to have been in the company, went a day's journey." (Luke 2:44.)*

In early Israel, distance was usually measured by the length of time required to walk it. The distance Abraham hiked with his son Isaac from Beersheba in the Negev up to the land of Moriah (the Temple Mount in Jerusalem) was a three days' journey. (See Gen. 22:4.) There was a "three days' journey" between Jacob and Laban (Gen. 30:36), and Laban pursued Jacob to Mount Gilead a "seven days' journey" (Gen. 31:23). It took an "eleven days' journey" from Mount Horeb to Kadesh-barnea. (Deut. 1:2.) Jonah traveled into the city (district?) of Nineveh "a day's journey." (Jonah 3:4.)

Over a hundred years ago, after a trip to the Holy Land, Mark Twain wrote that "all distances in the East are measured by hours, not miles. A good horse will walk three miles an hour over nearly any kind of a road; therefore, an hour, here, always stands for three miles."[2] The present writer, who has walked from Dan to Beersheba, and from the Jordan River to the Mediterranean, and from Jerusalem to the Red Sea—the length and breadth of the Holy Land—confirms the same standard measure for people. Forty different walks in all types of terrain have proved that three miles an hour is a constant average, even with animals. If we assume seven to eight hours of journeying per day, the dis-

tance covered would be possibly twenty to twenty-five miles a day.

Joseph and Mary took the twelve-year-old Jesus to Jerusalem for the Passover celebration. On the return trip to Nazareth, they went "a day's journey" before discovering that Jesus was not in their company. If they were traveling via Samaria, they could have reached nearly to the ancient site of Shiloh (approximately twenty-five miles north of Jerusalem). Or if via the Jordan Valley, they could have reached Jericho. It would have been a worrisome and wearisome trek back to Jerusalem again to find Jesus, who had already for three days been about his "Father's business." (Luke 2:49.)

On one occasion during his ministry, Jesus, walking from Jerusalem to Galilee, passed through Samaria. He stopped at Jacob's Well to drink and rest while his disciples went into the nearby town for food. John 4:6 says he was "wearied with his journey, [and] sat thus on the well: and it was about the sixth hour." It would probably have been the sixth hour (noontime) *on the second day of the journey* since Jacob's Well is about forty miles north of Jerusalem.

A "sabbath day's journey" was the distance allowable to walk on the Sabbath, a rabbinical restriction based on the Mosaic injunction "Let no man go out of his place on the seventh day." (Ex. 16:29.) The maximum distance specified was two thousand cubits (three thousand feet). It was about that distance from the city wall of Jerusalem to the Mount of Olives. (See Acts 1:12.)

By the early Roman period, some

Greek measures were also in use. The *furlong* or *stade* was about six hundred feet, the length of the race-track at Olympia. After Jesus' resurrection, two disciples walked "to a village called Emmaus, which was from Jerusalem about threescore furlongs" (Luke 24:13), which is about seven miles. (See also "Emmaus," in chapter 2).

"When they had rowed about five and twenty or thirty furlongs, they see Jesus walking on the sea." (John 6:19.) That distance in furlongs is fifteen to eighteen thousand feet, or three to four miles, right out in the middle of the lake — all the more impressive when they saw him walking on the water!

"Now Bethany was nigh unto Jerusalem, about fifteen furlongs off." (John 11:18.) That is one and a third miles, which is how far the town lies over the Mount of Olives from the walls of Jerusalem.

One other measure of distance is used in the New Testament: the Roman mile. "Whosoever shall compel thee to go a mile, go with him twain." (Matt. 5:41.) The Roman mile was familiar to all travelers in Jesus' day. The Romans had already begun their vast network of roads throughout the empire, which would eventually become the greatest road system the world had ever known. They placed milestones at regular intervals along the roads to constantly remind the populace of who ruled them. Hundreds of those milestones have been found dating back to Roman Palestine. The Roman mile was a thousand paces or about 4,860 feet — shorter than the modern mile.

*"A certain man went down from Jerusalem to Jericho." (Luke 10:30.)*

So begins one of the most familiar stories in all the world's literature, the parable of the good Samaritan. Without pause to reflect on the physical setting, most teachers and students of the Bible will immediately launch into a philosophical or didactic analysis of the text. However, in this case, as in most of the writings contained in the Bible, there is an understood geographical setting that underlies the story and events in it.

To the Jews, Jerusalem is the high point of temporal and spiritual life. The Holy City is situated in the high hills of Judaea. The New Testament contains the phrase "up to Jerusalem" or "up unto Jerusalem" twenty-two times. Westerners will often view any place north as "up north," whereas in the Holy Land the region around the Sea of Galilee, though north, is referred to as "down north," being lower in elevation.

So from the Galilee, the Jordan Valley, the Coastal Plains, or anywhere in the country, it was a journey *up* to Jerusalem. "When he was twelve years old, they went up to Jerusalem after the custom of the feast." (Luke 2:42.) "The Jews' passover was at hand, and Jesus went up to Jerusalem." (John 2:13.) "When he had thus spoken, he went before, ascending up to Jerusalem." (Luke 19:28.) "He was seen many days of them which came up with him from Galilee to Jerusalem." (Acts 13:31.) "Now when Festus was come into the province, after three days he ascended from Caesarea to Jerusalem." (Acts 25:1.)

5

The adverbs *up* and *down* may not register any particular importance to Westerners accustomed to driving vehicles in the modern world, but travel in the ancient world was arduous and fraught with dangers and concerns. Elevation differences in the Holy Land were remembered with every footstep, and biblical writers referred constantly, even automatically, to those differences.

When Jesus was in Cana of Galilee on one occasion, a nobleman from Capernaum came pleading for his dying son: "When [the nobleman] heard that Jesus was come out of Judaea into Galilee, he went unto him, and besought him that he would come *down,* and heal his son. . . . The nobleman saith unto him, Sir, come *down* ere my child die." And later, "as he was now going *down,* his servants met him, and told him, saying, Thy son liveth." (John 4:47–51; italics added.) Cana lies a few miles north of Nazareth at an elevation of about seven hundred feet *above* sea level, whereas Capernaum is situated along the northern shore of the Sea of Galilee, at nearly seven hundred feet *below* sea level.

Returning to the parable of the good Samaritan, we note that although it is only a story, it is true to all geographical detail, especially the beginning note that the man had to walk "*down* from Jerusalem to Jericho." Jerusalem is about two thousand five hundred feet above sea level, and Jericho, at eight hundred feet below sea level, is the lowest town on the globe.

Just as biblical writers referred to travel to Jerusalem as "up," they referred to travel from Jerusalem as "down." Jesus "went down with them, and came to Nazareth." (Luke 2:51.) "Then Philip went down to the city of Samaria, and preached Christ unto them." (Acts 8:5.) Philip journeyed in "the way that goeth down from Jerusalem unto Gaza." (Acts 8:26.) "As Peter passed throughout all quarters, he came down also to the saints which dwelt at Lydda." (Acts 9:32.) Herod Agrippa "went down from Judaea to Caesarea." (Acts 12:19.)

The reference to Philip going *down* to the city of Samaria is most interesting. Samaria is about forty-five miles north of Jerusalem and high in the hills. Nevertheless, it is still over one thousand feet lower in elevation than Jerusalem. The reference to descent, however, is likely more than mere physical elevation. Just as modern Israelis regard those who leave the land of Israel as *yordim* — those who go down — and those who immigrate to the land as *olim* — those who come up — so Jerusalem represents the pinnacle, the highest point. To go anywhere else after Jerusalem is to go down from the Holy City.

*"Every valley shall be filled, and every mountain and hill shall be brought low; and the crooked shall be made straight, and the rough ways shall be made smooth."*
*(Luke 3:5.)*

The topography of the Holy Land is extremely diverse, as evidenced by the preceding descriptions of elevation differences. From west to east, one encounters a flat coastal plain, then low hills, then high hills, and finally a deep rift valley. From north to south, there is hill country,

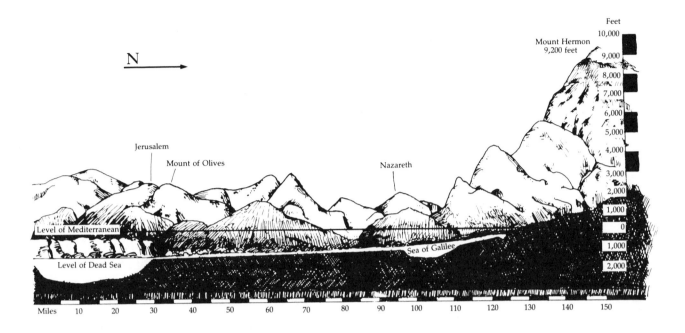

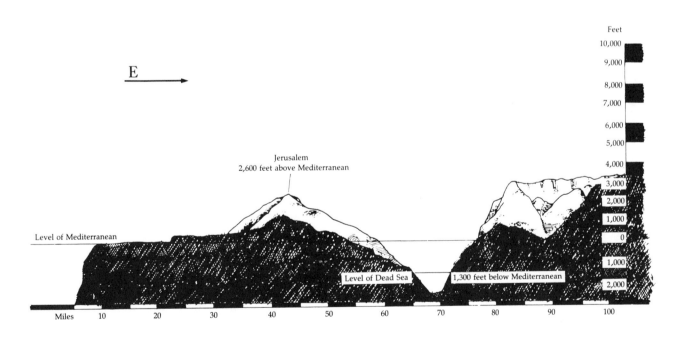

Map 1

*Upper crosscut:* The Holy Land from south to north. *Lower crosscut:* The Holy Land from west to east.

then a broad level valley, then more hill country, then flat and mountainous desert lands. There are gently undulating grasslands, but there is also steep, precipitous terrain: "The herd ran violently down a steep place into the lake, and were choked." (Luke 8:33.)

The Holy Land features a considerable variety of landscapes. From Mount Hermon, snow-covered much of the year, to the borders of some of the earth's great deserts, the land from one end to the other is a study in contrast. Since the hills lead downward in all directions, the land is naturally crisscrossed with wadis. Wadis are riverbeds that are dry most of the year but filled with turbulent water during the rains. Many of them form oases. Since the native stone is porous limestone, it is also pockmarked with caves: "They wandered in deserts, and in mountains, and in dens and caves of the earth." (Heb. 11:38.)

Israel has a long, straight Mediterranean coastline where ages of currents have washed up onto the land vast stretches of fine sand. The sands were compared to the children of Israel, "as the sand which is by the sea shore innumerable." (Heb. 11:12.)

From the coastal plain inland and eastward, the hill country begins. Judaea is referred to as "hill country." (Luke 1:39, 65.) Two Greek terms are used interchangeably for hill or mountain—*bounos* and *oros,* the latter being used much more frequently than the former. English *mount* is used to specify a certain mountain. The singular term refers numerous times to the Mount of Olives, but also occasionally to Mount Sinai, the Mount of Transfigura-

tion, and Mount Zion.

New Testament authors wrote five times of a "high mountain." High mountains are, of course, defined in terms of ancient Jewish geographic mentality, not in comparison with the American Rockies or European Alps. The mountains are "high" compared to the surrounding terrain. For instance, when the scripture says, "The devil taketh him up into an exceeding high mountain" (Matt. 4:8), the summit of the fault escarpment above the Jordan Rift Valley floor near Jericho is acceptable as an "exceedingly high mountain" from the Judaeans' point of view.

New Testament authors also wrote three times of a "mountain apart." Reference to a "mountain apart" usually signifies an occasion when Jesus needed to get away from the crowds to spiritually rejuvenate himself or to participate in some private communication with his Father. "When he had sent the multitudes away, he went up into a mountain apart to pray." (Matt. 14:23.) "After six days Jesus taketh Peter, James, and John his brother, and bringeth them up into an high mountain apart." (Matt. 17:1.) "He went out into a mountain to pray, and continued all night in prayer." (Luke 6:12.) "He departed again into a mountain himself alone." (John 6:15.)

Besides the Mount of Olives, Mount Sinai, and Mount Zion, there are a few other specific mountains referred to in the New Testament. The traditional Mount of Temptation stands high above old Jericho, which the conquering Israelite armies of Joshua destroyed. From that vantage point, Jesus could only have *envisioned* the

*Top left and right:* Examples of milestones from Roman Palestine. The right photograph shows a milestone found along the Via Maris (International Highway) near Capernaum. *Center left:* Students from Brigham Young University walking the route of the Roman road from Jerusalem down to Jericho. *Center right:* Mount Tabor—the traditional Mount of Transfiguration, a "high mountain apart." (Matt. 17:1.) *Bottom left:* Journeying through the desolate Judaean Wilderness. *Bottom right:* Plain of Bethsaida—site of the feeding of the five thousand—"a desert place" with "much grass." (Luke 9:10; John 6:10.)

kingdoms of the world, as there is no grandeur whatever of worldly kingdoms visible from that site. The traditional Mount of Transfiguration (Mount Tabor) is a veritable "high mountain apart" from the surrounding hills in the eastern Jezreel Valley (though the other candidate, Mount Hermon, certainly fits the description also). The Samaritan woman at Jacob's Well observed that "our fathers worshipped in this mountain; and ye say, that in Jerusalem is the place where men ought to worship." (John 4:20.) "This mountain" is Mount Gerizim, which was then and is now the holy mountain of the Samaritans, rival of the Jews' Mount Moriah.

Another unnamed mountain was the site of a post-resurrection appearance by Jesus to his apostles: "Then the eleven disciples went away into Galilee, into a mountain where Jesus had appointed them." (Matt. 28:16.) This could be Mount Arbel, a high point overlooking the whole Sea of Galilee region where Jesus' teaching ministry had been accomplished. Mount Arbel has a grand panorama from Mount Hermon to the volcanic cones of the Golan, to the Yarmuk canyon cutting through the Decapolis, around to Mount Tabor in the southwest, and directly behind to the Horns of Hittin, an extinct volcano looming up on the west. There, on the secluded edge of the twelve-hundred-foot precipice, Jesus could have inspired his leading disciples with their commission to take the gospel to all the world.

Jesus prophesied of tragic war that would involve Jerusalem not long after he left the earth. Among other things he warned, "Let them which are in Judaea flee to the mountains; and let them which are in the midst of it depart out." (Luke 21:21.) At first glance, speaking of the inhabitants of Judaea fleeing to the mountains may be puzzling, especially since they already live in the tops of the mountains. But the other side of the parallelism may help: "Let them which are in the midst of it depart out."

Jesus may be suggesting that Judaeans flee eastward through the wilderness, the usual course of flight, and find safety in the mountain refuges on the edge of the wilderness, like Masada, where David had hid from the armies of Saul a millennium before.

## "What went ye out into the wilderness to see?" (Matt. 11:7.)

As we have seen, Jesus retired to the mountains for seclusion and solitude. Desert areas likewise provided opportunity for revitalizing introspection and communion. Moses spent years in the Sinai Wilderness preparing for his task of delivering Israel, and then the delivered Israelites spent forty years preparing to enter their promised land. The Judaean Desert and desolate Rift Valley east of Jericho was the setting for the ministry of John the Baptist. He was "in the deserts till the day of his shewing unto Israel." (Luke 1:80.) Then "the word of God came unto John the son of Zacharias in the wilderness" (Luke 3:2), and "in those days came John the Baptist, preaching in the wilderness of Judaea" (Matt. 3:1).

Jesus began his ministry by baptism in the Jordan "and immediately the Spirit driveth him into the wilderness." (Mark

1:12.) There in the silent and lonely desert, he prepared to face his mortal assignment. But preparation is not a one-time necessity. Even the Lord desired periodic refreshing. "He departed thence by ship into a desert place apart." (Matt. 14:13.) "They departed into a desert place by ship privately." (Mark 6:32.) "He withdrew himself into the wilderness, and prayed." (Luke 5:16.)

There are indeed desolate regions of wasteland in the Near East, notably the Sahara and parts of the Arabian Desert. There is no place in the land of Jesus, however, that could properly be designated utter wasteland. All desert lands in Israel and the Sinai have a surprising amount of animal life and flora.

One point does need to be clarified. The words *desert* and *wilderness* are used interchangeably in English translations or versions of the Bible, both in the Old and New Testaments. All Hebrew and Greek words used signify deserted or uninhabited places. The most frequently used Hebrew word is *midbar*, which is a tract for pasturing flocks. On the other hand, *yeshimon* is the wild, harsh desertland. The Judaean Desert fits both descriptions — the higher elevations are mostly uninhabited and are used for herding, but the lower sections, nearer the Dead Sea, are barren, forbidding regions. In Greek, *eremia* and *eremos* are derived from the same root and are used interchangeably for uninhabited pastureland *or* wasteland.

When Joseph's brothers wanted to kill Joseph but decided instead to throw him into a pit, the account says, "Shed no blood, but cast him into this pit that is in the wilderness." (Gen. 37:22.) The brothers were shepherding in the Dothan Valley, which is fertile agricultural and pastoral land just south of the great Jezreel Valley. The word "wilderness" used here — *midbar* in Hebrew — is not out of place but fits perfectly the definition of unsettled pasturage area.

One important event recorded by all four Gospel writers is the feeding of "five thousand men, beside women and children." (Matt. 14:21.) The apostles were sent out on missions, and "when they were returned, . . . he took them, and went aside privately into a desert place belonging to the city called Bethsaida. . . . And when the day began to wear away, then came the twelve, and said unto him, Send the multitude away, that they may go into the towns and country round about, and lodge, and get victuals: for we are here in a desert place" (Luke 9:10, 12); that is, we are in a solitary or uninhabited place.

Matthew records the disciples' question, "Whence should we have so much bread in the wilderness, as to fill so great a multitude?" (Matt. 15:33.) John adds, "Now there was much grass in the place." (John 6:10.) Most people do not envision a desert having grass, but here again the "desert" is not wasteland, but uninhabited pasturage area. In his Hebrew translation of the New Testament, Franz Delitszch used the word *midbar* here.

We can conclude, then, that desert or wilderness is found in all parts of the land, wherever no sizeable human population exists. It can range from barren land to land used sometimes for grazing flocks and herds.

## "Go ye therefore into the highways." (Matt. 22:9.)

One thing yet remains to be mentioned about the geographical features of the Holy Land: the man-made highways. Matthew, Mark, and Luke all refer in one instance to "highways," but the usual term for a travel route in the New Testament is "way." Some Roman roads we know; others we can only speculate on their course.

The following roads are referred to in the specified passages:

1. International Highway, the Via Maris. (See Matt. 2:19–23; 4:15.)

2. Through Huleh Valley to Caesarea Philippi. (See Mark 8:27.)

3. Way to Capernaum. (See Mark 9:33–34.)

4. Jerusalem to Galilee, via Samaria. (See John 4:3–6, 40, 43.) Galilee to Jerusalem, via Samaria. (See Luke 9:51–53.)

5. Jericho to Jerusalem, via Judaean Desert (or vice versa). (See Matt. 20:17; Mark 10:32, 46; Luke 10:31; 18:35.)

6. Bethphage over Mount of Olives to Jerusalem. (See Matt. 21:8; Mark 11:1.)

7. Jerusalem to Emmaus. (See Luke 24:13, 32, 35.)

8. Jerusalem to Gaza. (See Acts 8:26, 36, 39.)

9. Way (through Golan) to Damascus. (See Acts 9:17, 27; 26:13.)

There are evidences of the Via Maris, both in engraved inscriptions and archaeological remains, and some are found along the way to Capernaum. Most indication of the routes of Roman roads comes from hundreds of milestones found. Short sections of the Jericho-Jerusalem Road through the Judaean Desert and the Jerusalem-Coastal Road via the Elah Valley are still visible today.

### NOTES

1. *The Life and Times of Jesus the Messiah* (Grand Rapids, Michigan: William B. Eerdmans Publishing Company, 1972), 212.

2. *The Innocents Abroad* (New York: The Heritage Press, 1962), 398.

# REGIONS AND SETTLEMENTS IN THE HOLY LAND

*"Whithersoever he entered, into villages, or cities, or country, they . . . besought him." (Mark 6:56.)*

There were several types of settlements in New Testament times. A city (Greek, *polis*) usually refers to a larger town. The Greek term *kome* designated a small town or village. Jerusalem is consistently presented as a city and was indeed the largest walled city in the country. However, other towns, large or small, are also described in the King James Bible as "cities":

Arimathaea: "He was of Arimathaea, a city of the Jews." (Luke 23:51.)

Azotus: "Philip was found at Azotus: and passing through he preached in all the cities, till he came to Caesarea" (Acts 8:40) — Philip taught at least in Gaza, Azotus, Joppa, and Caesarea.

Bethlehem: "Joseph also went up . . . into Judaea, unto the city of David, which is called Bethlehem." (Luke 2:4.)

"For unto you is born this day in the city of David a Saviour." (Luke 2:11.)

Bethsaida: "He took them, and went aside privately into a desert place belonging to the city called Bethsaida." (Luke 9:10.)

"Philip was of Bethsaida, the city of Andrew and Peter." (John 1:44.)

Caesarea: "Agrippa was come, and Bernice . . . with the chief captains, and principal men of the city." (Acts 25:23.)

Capernaum: "He entered into a ship, and passed over, and came into his own city." (Matt. 9:1.)

"[He] came down to Capernaum, a city of Galilee, and taught them." (Luke 4:31.)

Ephraim: "[Jesus] went thence unto a country near to the wilderness, into a city called Ephraim." (John 11:54.)

Nain: "And it came to pass the day after, that he went into a city called Nain." (Luke 7:11; see also v. 12.)

Joppa: "I [Peter] was in the city of Joppa praying." (Acts 11:5.)

Nazareth: "The angel Gabriel was sent from God unto a city of Galilee, named

Nazareth." (Luke 1:26.)

"They returned into Galilee, to their own city Nazareth." (Luke 2:39.)

Samaria: "Philip went down to the city of Samaria, and preached. . . . And there was great joy in that city." (Acts 8:5, 8.)

Sarepta: "Unto none of them was Elias sent, save unto Sarepta, a city of Sidon." (Luke 4:26.)

Sychar: "Then cometh he to a city of Samaria, which is called Sychar." (John 4:5; see also vv. 8, 28, 30, 39.)

Others: "Then began he to upbraid the cities [Capernaum, Chorazin, and Bethsaida] wherein most of his mighty works were done." (Matt. 11:20.)

"Turning the cities of Sodom and Gomorrha into ashes . . . " (2 Pet. 2:6.)

The following places are specifically described as a "town" or "village":

Bethany: "A certain man was sick, named Lazarus, of Bethany, the town of Mary and her sister Martha." (John 11:1; see also v. 30.)

Bethlehem: "Christ cometh of the seed of David, and out of the town of Bethlehem." (John 7:42.)

Bethphage: "Go ye into the village over against you, and straightway ye shall find an ass tied." (Matt. 21:2.)

Bethsaida: "He cometh to Bethsaida. . . . And he took the blind man by the hand, and led him out of the town. . . . And he sent him away to his house, saying, Neither go into the town, nor tell it to any in the town." (Mark 8:22–26.)

Caesarea Philippi: "Jesus went out, and his disciples, into the towns of Caesarea Philippi." (Mark 8:27.)

Emmaus: "Two of them went that same day to a village called Emmaus." (Luke 24:13; see also v. 28.)

Looking at such a listing of "cities" and "towns" or "villages" raises a question about the use of the terms *polis* and *kome*. Jerusalem, Samaria, and the hellenized coastal towns merit the designation "city," as they were large, influential, and walled (even though during the *Pax Romana*, there was less justification for fortifying cities with protective walls). On the other hand, it is unlikely that Nazareth, Bethlehem, Nain, Bethsaida, Arimathaea, Sychar, and Ephraim deserved to be called "cities," as they were small, unwalled, and relatively insignificant places at the time of Jesus. Bethsaida and Bethlehem were called cities by some Gospel writers and towns by others. Apparently, the terms *city* and *town* were used interchangeably.

The term *country* appears frequently in the New Testament. On a few occasions the term refers to a foreign land, as in the wise men departing "into their own country another way" (Matt. 2:12), and in an allusion to Barnabas, the Levite disciple, who came from "the country of Cyprus" (Acts 4:36). Mention of a "far country" in the parables (Matt. 21:33; 25:14; Mark 12:1; Luke 15:13; 19:12; 20:9) may refer to distant

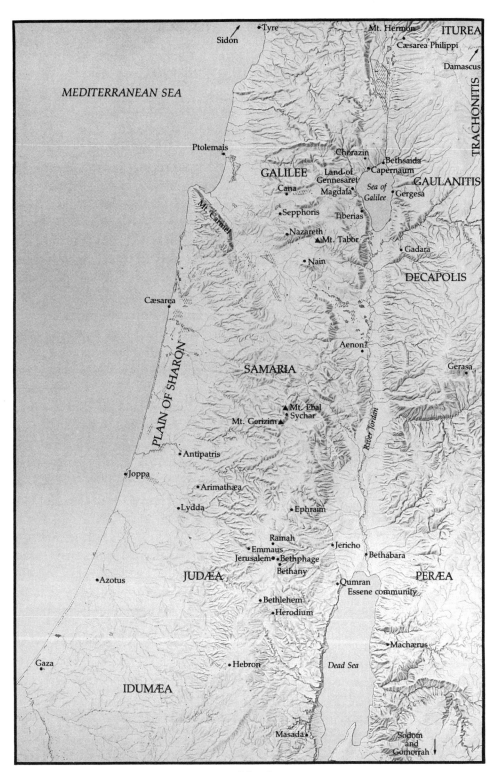

Map 2

The Holy Land with New Testament sites. Large capitals indicate regions.

parts of the land of the Jews as well as to distant, foreign countries.

Most uses of the term, however, refer simply to land or countryside outside of the settlement: "He was come to the other side into the country of the Gergesenes." (Matt. 8:28.) "They came over unto the other side of the sea, into the country of the Gadarenes." (Mark 5:1.) "Whithersoever he entered, into villages, or cities, or country, they laid the sick in the streets." (Mark 6:56.) "After that he appeared . . . unto two of them, as they walked, and went into the country." (Mark 16:12.) "They that fed the swine fled, and told it in the city, and in the country." (Mark 5:14.) "Send the multitudes away, that they may go into the towns and country round about." (Luke 9:12.)

*"Arise, and take the young child and his mother, and go into the land of Israel." (Matt. 2:20.)*

The land of Jesus is presented with three different appellations in the New Testament: Canaan, the land of Israel, and the land of the Jews. The people of Israel, after their forty-year sojourn in the wilderness, entered the Egyptian province called Canaan, with geographical boundaries including most of Lebanon and all of present-day Israel.

Canaan (or Chanaan in two places) is mentioned only three times in the New Testament, twice in connection with the former history of Israel. "Now there came a dearth over all the land of Egypt and Chanaan." (Acts 7:11.) "When he had destroyed seven nations in the land of Cha-

naan, he divided their land." (Acts 13:19.) The other occurrence of the term refers to "a woman of Canaan" (Matt. 15:22) living along the Phoenician coast. Elsewhere the woman is called "a Greek, a Syro-phenician by nation." (Mark 7:26.)

Though the term *Canaanite* appears twice, it refers to an apostle named "Simon the Canaanite" (Matt. 10:4; Mark 3:18), elsewhere called "Simon Zelotes" (Luke 6:15; Acts 1:13). The word *Canaanite*, or *Cananaean* in this case, refers not to nationality or geographical provenance but derives from the Aramaic word *qan'an*, meaning zealous. Simon may have been a Zealot, which was a group active in opposing Roman rule.

Only Matthew designates the land as "the land of Israel." The title passage for this section shows the divine command to Joseph to return with his wife, Mary, and the child, Jesus, to their homeland. The next verse reflects his simple obedience: "He arose, and took the young child and his mother, and came into the land of Israel." (Matt. 2:21.)

One other descriptive title for the country is recorded in the testimony of Peter, "We are witnesses of all things which he did both in the land of the Jews, and in Jerusalem." (Acts 10:39.)

*"There followed him great multitudes of people from Galilee, and from Decapolis, and from Jerusalem, and from Judaea, and from beyond Jordan." (Matt. 4:25.)*

This phrase in Matthew lists many of the regions of the Holy Land. The term *region* itself is used ten times with a place

16

name in the King James Version of the New Testament. "Then went out to him Jerusalem, and all Judaea, and all the region round about Jordan." (Matt. 3:5.) "Immediately his fame spread abroad throughout all the region round about Galilee." (Mark 1:28.)

The Gospels and Acts, however, use the term *coasts* eleven times, referring to the borders or boundaries of a region. In most cases, the use of the word *coasts* could not possibly have any connection to shorelines, as the localities are inland. "Then Herod . . . slew all the children that were in Bethlehem, and in all the coasts thereof." (Matt. 2:16.) "Jesus came into the coasts of Caesarea Philippi." (Matt. 16:13.) "He departed from Galilee, and came into the coasts of Judaea beyond Jordan." (Matt. 19:1.) " . . . first unto them of Damascus, and at Jerusalem, and throughout all the coasts of Judaea." (Acts 26:20.)

At the death of Herod the Great, Herod's will stipulated that three of his sons would rule his kingdom: Archelaus as ethnarch (literally, "ruler of the people") over Judaea and Samaria, Antipas as tetrarch ("ruler of a fourth [of the country]") of Galilee and Peraea, and Philip as tetrarch of several regions to the north and east of Galilee. Some ten years later, the Romans deposed the tyrant Archelaus and installed a series of Roman governors to rule the middle of the country. John the Baptist began his ministry "in the fifteenth year of the reign of Tiberius Caesar, Pontius Pilate being governor of Judaea, and Herod [Antipas] being tetrarch of Galilee, and his brother Philip tetrarch of Ituraea

and of the region of Trachonitis." (Luke 3:1.)

## REGIONS OF THE HOLY LAND

*Galilee (see map, page 15, for location of this and all the following regions)*

There are over fifty references in the Gospels to Galilee as a region, the first mention being Joseph's return from Egypt with Mary and Jesus to live in the northernmost region of the land of Israel: "When he heard that Archelaus did reign in Judaea . . . , he was afraid to go thither: . . . he turned aside into the parts of Galilee." (Matt. 2:22.)

Jesus' ministry begins with a geographical note: "Then cometh Jesus from Galilee to Jordan unto John, to be baptized of him." (Matt. 3:13; see Mark 1:14.) And then "Jesus went about all Galilee, teaching in their synagogues." (Matt. 4:23.) Important towns of Galilee in Jesus' ministry included "Nazareth of Galilee" (Matt. 21:11), "Capernaum, a city of Galilee" (Luke 4:31), "Cana of Galilee" (John 2:1), and "Bethsaida of Galilee" (John 12:21).

One of the most important towns in Galilee was Sepphoris (located about three miles northwest of Nazareth), where Herod Antipas resided prior to making Tiberias the capital of Galilee. Since Sepphoris is not mentioned in the New Testament, few people have heard of it. Jesus may have taught there since he went throughout all of Galilee.

All but one of Jesus' apostles were Galilaeans (Judas Iscariot was perhaps a Judaean.) When Jesus departed into heaven from the Mount of Olives, two men in white apparel asked, "Ye men of Galilee, why stand ye gazing up into heaven." (Acts 1:11.)

The speech of Galilaeans was apparently distinct from their fellow countrymen. A young girl at Caiaphas's palace in Jerusalem accused Peter, "Surely thou art one of them: for thou art a Galilaean, and thy speech agreeth thereto." (Mark 14:70.) Matthew adds, "Surely thou also art one of them; for thy speech bewrayeth thee [Greek: reveals you]." (Matt. 26:73.) At the celebration of Pentecost after the Lord's resurrection, the thousands that had gathered in Jerusalem from all the Mediterranean world were amazed and marveled at the linguistic phenomenon they had witnessed, "saying one to another, Behold, are not all these which speak Galilaeans?" (Acts 2:7.)

How did Judaeans regard those from Galilee? Speaking to Jews of Judaea on one occasion, Jesus asked, "Suppose ye that these Galilaeans were sinners above all the Galilaeans?" (Luke 13:2), inferring that Judaeans looked with condescension, even disdain, upon Galilaeans. Certainly most of those revered personalities of former times had come from Judaea, and most Judaeans now expected nothing good from Galilee. "Shall Christ come out of Galilee? . . . Search, and look: for out of Galilee ariseth no prophet." (John 7:41, 52.)

When the region of Galilee first appeared in historical records (in the annals of Pharaoh Thutmose III), it was not Jewish but a conglomeration of Amorites and Canaanites. Perhaps this is the rationale behind the expression "Galilee of the gen-

tiles" (Matt. 4:15) or "Galilee of the nations" (Isa. 9:1; Greek, *Galilaia ton ethnon*).

When Israelites dominated the region, they retained the title "Galilee," referring to lands from the Litani River in southern Lebanon south to the Jezreel Valley, which separates Galilee from the province of Samaria. Topographically the region is divided into "Upper" and "Lower" Galilee, distinguished by elevation. Matthew (4:15) quotes Isaiah (9:1) identifying Galilee as the tribal regions of Zebulun and Naphtali. Nazareth was in Zebulun, and the Sea of Galilee and surrounding settlements were in Naphtali.

## Decapolis

"There followed him great multitudes of people from Galilee, and from Decapolis." (Matt. 4:25.) The Decapolis was an association of ten Greek cities (*deca* = ten, and *polis* = city) to the east and south of Galilee. The cities were Greek in the sense of having a predominantly Greek or hellenized culture.

In the New Testament, the Decapolis is mentioned two additional times. (See Mark 5:20; 7:31.) Jesus traveled and performed miracles among the Greeks, some of whom became disciples. The ten cities included Damascus, Raphana, Dion, Hippos (Hebrew, *Susita*), Gadara, Scythopolis (formerly called Beth-shean), Pella, Gerasa (today's Jerash), Philadelphia (today's Amman), and Abila or Canatha.

## Ituraea and Trachonitis

"Philip [was] tetrarch of Ituraea and of the region of Trachonitis." (Luke 3:1.) When Herod the Great died, his son Philip

18

was granted control of the lands north and east of Galilee, including the slopes of Mount Hermon and the Lebanese Beq'a. This area comprised Ituraea and Trachonitis. Important towns were Caesarea Philippi, at the foot of Hermon, and Bethsaida, on the northeast shore of the Sea of Galilee. South of Ituraea were regions called Ulatha and Gaulanitis (today's Golan), and south of Trachonitis were Batanaea and Auranitis.

## Samaria

"He must needs go through Samaria." (John 4:4.) The northern boundary of Samaria in Jesus' day was the Jezreel Valley. The southern boundary was arbitrarily demarcated, however, since there is no geological or topographical feature that separates the hill country of Samaria from the hill country of Judaea. The border point, according to Jewish historian Josephus, was a small village called Anuathu Borcaeus, just north of the Lebonah Valley in the hill country of Ephraim.

Jesus journeyed back and forth between Galilee and Judaea, often walking through Samaria, which is surprising considering the Judaeans' derisive attitude toward Samaritans. The Jews regarded them as genealogical half-breeds and historical antagonists: "The Jews have no dealings with the Samaritans." (John 4:9.) One of the Jews' ultimate curses was to pronounce someone a Samaritan: "Say we not well that thou art a Samaritan, and hast a devil?" (John 8:48.)

But Jesus did not avoid Samaritans. In fact, he once stayed for several days in Samaritan villages and taught them. Just as the story of Jonah taught former-day Israelites that salvation was for all of God's children, that all must have a chance to hear and repent, so Jesus pointedly illustrated God's concern for all peoples despite local prejudice. He immortalized the Samaritan people by his parable about a man (a Jew) assaulted along the Jericho road: "A certain Samaritan, as he journeyed, came where he was: and when he saw him, he had compassion on him." (Luke 10:33.) The only one of the ten lepers Jesus healed who came back to express gratitude was a Samaritan. (See Luke 17:16.)

The first recorded instance of Jesus openly declaring to anyone that he was the Messiah was to a Samaritan woman at Jacob's Well. (See John 4:5–26.) The woman could not contain her excitement and called the townspeople, who eagerly listened to Jesus. "Many of the Samaritans of that city believed on him," saying, "We have heard him ourselves, and know that this is indeed the Christ, the Saviour of the world." (John 4:39, 42.)

Jesus commissioned his disciples to preach the Gospel also in Samaria: "Ye shall be witnesses unto me both in Jerusalem, and in all Judaea, and in Samaria." (Acts 1:8.) So they went out and "testified and preached the word of the Lord . . . in many villages of the Samaritans." (Acts 8:25.) "At that time there was a great persecution against the church which was at Jerusalem; and they were all scattered abroad throughout the regions of Judaea and Samaria." (Acts 8:1.) Churches also grew in the land of the Samaritans. "Then had the churches rest throughout all Judaea and Galilee and Samaria." (Acts 9:31.)

## Coastal Plain

"All that dwelt at Lydda and Saron [the Sharon Plain] saw him, and turned to the Lord." (Acts 9:35.) This is the only general reference to coastal plains in the New Testament record, which was to feature prominently in the growth of the early Church. (More detail on individual sites appears later in this chapter.) When Peter performed a miracle at Lydda, people from all parts of the Sharon Plain enlisted in the Christian cause.

## Judaea

"It is evident that our Lord sprang out of Juda." (Heb. 7:14.) New Testament events occurred in two regions of Judaea: "the wilderness of Judaea" (Matt. 3:1) and "the hill country of Judaea" (Luke 1:65).

John the Baptist and Jesus both commenced their ministries in the wilderness, but their lives began in the hill country. "Mary arose in those days, and went into the hill country . . . into a city of Juda." (Luke 1:39.) Mary was visiting her relatives Zechariah and Elizabeth, parents of the prophet John the Baptist.

Tradition has long regarded En Kerem, a quaint village on the western outskirts of modern Jerusalem, as the birthplace of John. Another ancient tradition was revived by nineteenth-century biblical scholar Edward Robinson that Zechariah and Elizabeth lived in the village of Juttah, just south of Hebron, and that John was born in the south of Judaea.[1] It was one of the cities given to Aaron and his sons.

(See Josh. 21:13–16.) The tradition may be unlikely as the village of Juttah was situated in the region of Idumaea at that time.

In the New Testament, there seems to be constant intentional juxtaposition of Jerusalem and the rest of Judaea. Jerusalem was the capital, the chief and holy city, and merited preferential status or at least singular mention alongside any or all other places. Thus we see, "there went out unto him all the land of Judaea, and they of Jerusalem" (Mark 1:5), "a great multitude of people out of all Judaea and Jerusalem" (Luke 6:17). "Ye shall be witnesses unto me both in Jerusalem, and in all Judaea." (Acts 1:8.)

Jerusalem was synonymous with leadership. The headquarters of the early Christian Church was centered in the same place where centuries earlier God had chosen to place his name, where the Holy Temple had epitomized Judaic life for a millennium. Like the work of some of the old prophets, Jesus' most important work was performed and his life was given in Jerusalem. And though nearly all the members of the quorum of apostles were originally from Galilee, they clearly understood, too, that the center place of Zion, where the law and the word must go forth, was Jerusalem.

Though we hear of Bethlehem from Jesus' birth until Herod's slaying of the children, we hear of no other events in Bethlehem or in any other specific place south of Jerusalem in the New Testament. There is evidence, however, of proliferation of organized units of the Christian Church: "Then had the churches rest throughout all Judaea" (Acts 9:31); and

"That word . . . was published throughout all Judaea" (Acts 10:37). When Paul testified before Agrippa, he explained the course of his own teaching journeys. He "showed first unto them of Damascus, and at Jerusalem, and *throughout all the coasts of Judaea,* and then to the gentiles, that they should repent and turn to God." (Acts 26:20; italics added.)

## Jordan

"Then went out to him Jerusalem and all Judaea, and all the region round about Jordan, and were baptized of him in Jordan." (Matt. 3:5–6.) John baptized in the Jordan River east of Jericho at a place called Bethabara (see entry in this chapter). His ministry was actually located on the eastern shore of the river, in the region called Peraea. "Then cometh Jesus from Galilee to Jordan unto John, to be baptized of him" (Matt. 3:13); that is, Jesus left Galilee and walked south along the eastern side of the Jordan Valley into Peraea, opposite Jericho.

## Beyond Jordan

"He arose from thence, and cometh into the coasts of Judaea by the farther side of Jordan." (Mark 10:1.) The "farther side of Jordan" is the same phrase rendered seven other times as "beyond Jordan," meaning "across the Jordan" (*peran tou Jordanou*). The word *peran* is an adverb of place, and its cognate noun *Peraea* is known to stand by itself as a regional name, especially in the writings of Josephus. As we have seen, all directions given by Hebrew peoples are given as if standing looking east. Beyond Jordan,

then, would be on the eastern side of the river.

"There followed him great multitudes of people from Galilee, and from Decapolis, and from Jerusalem, and from Judaea, and from beyond Jordan [that is, from Peraea]." (Matt. 4:25.) Since all place names in the preceding passage are regional names (besides Jerusalem), it follows that "beyond Jordan" is also a regional name.

Both Galilee and Peraea were provinces ruled by Herod Antipas. Later, Herod Antipas would have John the Baptist incarcerated and put to death in the prison-fortress of Machaerus in southern Peraea.

## Idumaea

"Jesus withdrew himself with his disciples to the sea: and a great multitude from Galilee followed him, and from Judaea, and from Jerusalem, and from Idumaea, and from beyond Jordan; and they about Tyre and Sidon." (Mark 3:8.) Clearly the Gospel writers were impressed not only with the crowds gathering around Jesus, but also with the distances they had traveled to hear him. Those present at the Sea of Galilee from Idumaea had journeyed at least one hundred fifty miles to listen to this new teacher who spoke as one having authority.

At the time of Jesus, Idumaea was the territory stretching from just north of Hebron in the hill country to south of Beersheba in the Negev Desert. *Idumaea* is the English spelling of the Latin name for Edom, and Edomites had for several centuries lived also on the west of the

Rift Valley. Herod the Great was an Idumaean.

## INDIVIDUAL SITES IN GALILEE

*Caesarea Philippi (see map, page 15, for location of this and all the following settlements)*

At the southern foot of Mount Hermon, and at the headwaters of one source of the Jordan River, forty miles north of the Sea of Galilee, lies a town called in the Hellenistic period Panion or Panias. Herod the Great had erected there a white marble temple to the Greek god Pan. Inscribed niches still remain along the cliff face above the water source. When this town came under Herod Philip, he had it rebuilt, renaming it "Caesarea of Philip" to distinguish it from the Caesarea on the coast.

"When Jesus came into the coasts of Caesarea Philippi, he asked his disciples, saying, Whom do men say that I the Son of man am?" (Matt. 16:13.) They reported the circulating rumors that he was perhaps John the Baptist or Elijah or Jeremiah or some other prophet. Then Peter responded with forceful affirmation, "Thou art the Christ, the Son of the living God." (V. 16.) Jesus blessed Peter for listening to the voice of revelation from the Father.

Two geographical points may be made regarding this site. First, it is the only place in the country with a river flowing through the city. This is appropriate to what Jesus taught there: revelation must be continuous and flowing, like the river. Second, it provided a point of comparison for the Lord. As Hebrew writers loved to do, Jesus used paronomasia, a wordplay, on Peter's name. Said Jesus, "Thou art Peter [Greek, *petros,* or a rock], and upon this rock [Greek, *petra,* or rock mass] I will build my church." (V. 18.)

Because of the context of the statement, which immediately follows the Lord's blessing of Peter for receiving revelation, the rock—*petra*—in this case could signify revelation. Or, in mentioning rock, Jesus may have gestured to himself, meaning that he was the Rock of Salvation, the Stone of Israel. Jesus may well have been saying, "Peter, you are a rock (as the president of my church holding the keys of the kingdom), and upon the Rock of Salvation, which will give revelation, firmness, strength, and stability, I will build my church." The image was particularly appropriate for the location, as Caesarea Philippi sits at the foot of the most massive rock formation in the country.

### Capernaum

"Leaving Nazareth, he came and dwelt in Capernaum." (Matt. 4:13.) "He entered into a ship, and passed over, and came into his own city." (Matt. 9:1.) Capernaum was the last town in Herod Antipas's territory before crossing the Jordan, about two miles to the east, into Philip's territory. It would therefore have been a toll place or a collection point of custom or tax. Matthew Levi, one of the Romans' *publicani,* sat at receipt of custom or at the tax office and collected the hated taxes, at the same time drawing reproach from his fellow Jews.

Tribute money was also collected by town officials for the citizens of individual

*Top left:* Caesarea Philippi, located at the source of the Hermon River at the foot of Mount Hermon. *Top right:* Niches of a Herodian temple at Caesarea Philippi. *Center left:* Ruins of Capernaum in 1893. *Center right:* Reconstructed remains of a Capernaum synagogue. *Bottom left:* Motif of a date palm at the entrance to the Capernaum synagogue. *Bottom right:* Ruins of an ancient Chorazin synagogue, showing black basalt building stone.

towns. "When they were come to Capernaum, they that received tribute money came to Peter, and said, Doth not your master pay tribute?" (Matt. 17:24.) The collectors may have wondered, because priests and rabbis claimed exemption. Jesus gave instructions for finding the needed coin in the mouth of a fish, saying, "Lest we should offend them." (Matt. 17:27.) Was Jesus too poor to pay the money? Could he not have earned it by fishing? Considering who he was, Jesus condescended to pay the money but demonstrated his exalted status by fulfilling the law in a supernatural way, by a miracle without parallel.

Capernaum was a local crossroads near the International Highway, the Via Maris. Thus Roman soldiers were stationed there. "When Jesus was entered into Capernaum, there came unto him a centurion, beseeching him." (Matt. 8:5.) Capernaum was also a crossroads for those who sailed the lake. The town had a small port facility. Jesus' disciples "entered into a ship, and went over the sea toward Capernaum." (John 6:17.) "The people . . . also took shipping, and came to Capernaum, seeking for Jesus." (John 6:24.)

As evidenced by decades of excavation, especially recently, Capernaum was a major town built wholly of the local volcanic basalt and featuring a major synagogue (though after Jesus' century, limestone was imported to build a lovely white synagogue over the original basalt one). Jesus did more teaching and performed more miracles in Capernaum than in any other place throughout the land.

"Straightway on the sabbath day he entered into the synagogue, and taught." (Mark 1:21.) "These things said he in the synagogue, as he taught in Capernaum." (John 6:59.)

One of his greatest discourses concerned the "bread of life," which he gave in the synagogue at Capernaum—again a message appropriate to the place. At Capernaum, more grinding mills used for making bread have been found than at any other place in the country, leading some to believe that mills were manufactured in this Galilaean town and exported to others. Where these mills were produced for making bread, Jesus taught of spiritual bread, the partaking of which could nourish one to eternal life.

### Chorazin and Bethsaida

"Woe unto thee, Chorazin! woe unto thee, Bethsaida! for if the mighty works, which were done in you, had been done in Tyre and Sidon, they would have repented long ago in sackcloth and ashes." (Matt. 11:21.) Chorazin is situated in the hills two miles north of Capernaum in an area totally covered with black basalt; Bethsaida near the Jordan River's entrance to the Sea of Galilee at the northeast corner. They and Capernaum were included in the curses pronounced by Jesus. (See Matt. 11:23–24.) Jesus must have spent time and energy enough in Chorazin and Bethsaida to feel that the townspeople had been warned of impending judgments if they did not believe in him and repent of their sins.

We may take the curse of Jesus at face value. Today there is nothing but piles of rocks and partially restored ruins remaining at the sites of Chorazin and Capernaum, and nothing at all at the little fishing village of Bethsaida. Tiberias, on the other hand, was not mentioned in the curse, and it is still a thriving city today.

"Now Philip was of Bethsaida, the city of Andrew and Peter." (John 1:44.) Three of the twelve apostles were born in that fishing village. Near the town a blind man was healed in stages (see Mark 8:22–26), and in the Plain of Bethsaida the miraculous feeding of over five thousand people occurred (see Luke 9:10–17). Apparently a bigger Roman town of Bethsaida was established a couple of miles to the north along the Jordan River. It was called Bethsaida-Julias, named after a daughter of Augustus.

## Gennesaret

"When they were gone over, they came into the land of Gennesaret." (Matt. 14:34.) The Greek term *Gennesaret* is found twice in the New Testament as "the land of Gennesaret"—in the above passage and in its duplicate in Mark 6:53. It is also found once as a name for the Sea of Galilee. *Gennesaret* is the Greek adaptation of the Old Testament name *Chinnereth* (see Num. 34:11), and it is therefore related to modern *Kinneret*. In the title passage, Gennesaret refers to the cultivated plain on the west side of the Sea of Galilee.

## Magdala

"He sent away the multitude, and took ship, and came into the coasts of Magdala." (Matt. 15:39.) The town of Magdala, on the western shore of the Sea of Galilee, is mentioned one time only by this Hebrew name (*Migdol* means tower). The parallel passage in Mark mentions taking a ship to "the parts of Dalmanutha." (8:10.) Dalmanutha must be the same site as Magdala or be nearby.

There were at least five or six Marys in the New Testament, and one was from Magdala. Among the women disciples from Galilee who followed Jesus, Mary the Magdalene seems to have served in a leadership capacity. She is mentioned first in several listings of female followers (see, for example, Matt. 27:56; Luke 24:10), and she was first to see the resurrected Lord (see John 20:14, 18). Mary the Magdalene appears to have had some preeminent relationship with Jesus the Nazarene.

## Gergesa and Gadara

"When he was come to the other side into the country of the Gergesenes, there met him two possessed with devils." (Matt. 8:28.) Two discrepancies exist in the accounts of evil spirits being cast out in the Decapolis. Matthew indicates two men were possessed with devils, while Mark and Luke mention only one. Matthew has the incident taking place in Gergesa, whereas Mark and Luke both cite Gadara as the location of the miracle. Other Greek manuscripts have Gergesa, and some even claim Gerasa was where the demons were expelled.

The fact that swine were being herded and the phrase "other side of the sea" logically stipulate Gentile country in the Decapolis. When the devils possessed the large herd of swine, the swine ran down a steep place and were drowned in the lake. That alone disqualifies Gerasa (Jerash) as a possible location, as it is over thirty miles from the Sea of Galilee in the hill country of Gilead. Of the other two candidates, Gadara (Umm Qeis) seems also to be rather far for a herd to stampede to the shore of Galilee. Its slopes are several miles distant from the lake, with an intervening deep gorge and streambed of the Yarmuk River. Matthew's choice Gergesa (Kursi), now partially excavated and restored, is situated along the eastern shore of the Sea of Galilee less than a mile from the lake. It is the most likely site of this dramatic encounter between the forces of good and evil.

## Tiberias

"There came other boats from Tiberias." (John 6:23.) The city of Tiberias, named for the Roman emperor at the time, was established by Herod Antipas about A.D. 18, replacing his former Galilaean residence, Sepphoris. Tiberias was a Gentile city with no record of Jesus ever visiting or teaching there, though he may have passed through it when traveling south. The title passage and two others about the "sea of Tiberias" are the only mention of the city in the New Testament, all in the Gospel of John. (6:1; 21:1.) The city evidently had become prominent enough that the Sea of Galilee was sometimes called after the city.

## Cana

"There was a marriage in Cana of Galilee." (John 2:1.) So begins the story of Jesus' first recorded miracle, performed at a wedding feast in Cana. His second miracle of record was also performed at Cana—healing the son of a nobleman in Capernaum more than twenty miles away, showing that distance was no obstacle to his divine power. One of the twelve apostles, Nathanael, was also from Cana.

The traditional site of Cana is along the Nazareth-Tiberias highway, a small town now called in Arabic Kfar Kanna, literally the "village of Cana." Archaeology and toponymy (the study of place names) tell us, on the other hand, that Cana was located about eight miles north of Nazareth across the Bet Netofa Valley. There is a hill (inaccessible by automobile) with ancient ruins called in Arabic Kanna el-Jalil (Cana of Galilee.)

Jesus' presence at a marriage celebration shows that he was no social recluse (as were some Essenes, for example.) He enjoyed the company and association of others in wholesome human activities. The marriage itself might possibly have been that of one of Jesus' brothers or sisters. His mother Mary seems to have had some hosting role and turned to Jesus for help. Jesus himself was now over thirty years of age and would likely have married, which was customary for Jewish men to do in their late teens. Had he not been married, we would undoubtedly read of accusation after accusation against him, since marriage was number one of the God-given commandments. As we read of no objections to him teaching, he appears to have long since complied with one of the most important of the commandments.

## Nazareth

"He came and dwelt in a city called Nazareth: that it might be fulfilled which was spoken by the prophets, He shall be called a Nazarene." (Matt. 2:23.) The phrase "Jesus of Nazareth" occurs twenty times in the Gospels and Acts. Other people called him Jesus of Nazareth, Pilate ordered "Jesus of Nazareth" inscribed on the title-piece of the cross, and Jesus referred to himself as "Jesus of Nazareth" when appearing to Saul on the road to Damascus.

In the passage quoted above, Matthew sees fulfillment of a Messianic prophecy in Jesus' connection with Nazareth. We have no specific reference in biblical literature to prophets declaring that the Messiah would be a Nazarene, unless this is a paronomastic allusion to Isaiah 11:1. Isaiah foreshadowed that a "Branch" (*netzer*) would grow out of the root of Jesse—that is, from the Davidic line—and thus Jesus would be a Nazarene (*notzri*). Both Hebrew words come from the same root.

Nazareth was not an important town in Jesus' day. It is not mentioned in the Old Testament, or by Josephus, or in the Talmud. "Nazarene" was even a derisive term, as evidenced by Nathanael's remark, "Can there any good thing come out of Nazareth?" (John 1:46.)

Though the town was politically insignificant, it was not obscure in a geographical sense. Nazareth overlooks the great Jezreel Valley, the route of international traffic and news. A boy growing up in Nazareth could have learned of the affairs of men and nations while at the same time remaining distanced in a quiet provincial environment from the parade of worldliness. From his unimposing hometown milieu, Jesus took many lesson-symbols for his teachings: birds of the air, foxes in their holes, lilies in the fields, wine and olive presses, ploughs, grain, and watchtowers.

Of the thirty years before his ministry began, Jesus must have spent at least twenty-six in Nazareth and its environs. Though he was "subject unto" his parents most of those years (Luke 2:51), yet we wonder about his activities and work during his early years: who were his friends? what did he do? where did he travel?

After age thirty, near the beginning of his ministry elsewhere, "he came to Nazareth, where he had been brought up: and, as his custom was, he went into the synagogue on the sabbath day, and stood up for to read." (Luke 4:16.) The ensuing scene constitutes the most detailed description from antiquity of an ancient synagogue service. Jesus quoted a familiar Messianic prophecy from the scroll of Isaiah (see 61:1–2), closed it up, and then sat down to give commentary. The commentary was pure and simple: the scripture was being fulfilled by him.

Knowing what their reaction would be as they incredulously puzzled over who this hometown boy was claiming to be, he gave them to understand that their disbelief would obstruct any miracles on their behalf, and he expressed the axiom, "No prophet is accepted in his own country." (Luke 4:24.) After inciting them by saying that other prophets in the northern regions of the land, namely Elijah and Elisha, had also been unable to invoke mi-

*Top left:* Excavating the ruins of Scythopolis, capital of the Decapolis. *Top right:* Unexcavated ruins of Cana. *Center left:* Village of Nazareth, photographed in 1869. *Center right:* Example of "a city that is set on an hill" (Matt. 5:14) in Samaria. *Bottom left:* Sychar and Jacob's Well in the hill country of Samaria, between Mount Gerizim (left) and Mount Ebal (right). *Bottom right:* Drawing water from Jacob's Well, photographed in 1869.

raculous blessings on their own unbelieving people, the pious synagogue attenders of Nazareth led Jesus out to a nearby hill and tried to cast him off to his death. He escaped and went down to continue his ministry at Capernaum.

To the above axiom, Mark added, "A prophet is not without honour, but in his own country, and among his own kin, and in his own house." (Mark 6:4.) The verse suggests that some of Jesus' own relatives and family members did not accept at that time his claim to divinity.

*Nain*

"It came to pass the day after, that he went into a city called Nain." (Luke 7:11.) The day before his arrival at Nain, Jesus had been with his disciples in Capernaum. He had had a rigorous hike uphill of more than twenty-five miles to get to Nain "the day after."

Nain was (and still is) a small village at the northern foot of Mount Moreh in the eastern Jezreel Valley. Jesus stopped a funeral procession there and raised the only child of a widow from the dead, the very same thing the prophet Elisha had done centuries before on the other side of the mountain. (See 2 Kgs. 4.)

## INDIVIDUAL SITES IN SAMARIA

*Sychar, Jacob's Well (see map, page 15, for location of this and all the following settlements)*

"Then cometh he to a city of Samaria, which is called Sychar, near to the parcel of ground that Jacob gave to his son Joseph. Now Jacob's well was there." (John 4:5–6.) John is the only Gospel writer to record a journey north from Jerusalem to Galilee, where Jesus stopped at Jacob's Well.

Upon returning from his twenty-year residence in Mesopotamia, Jacob settled on a parcel of ground he purchased from local inhabitants to the east of the city of Shechem (see Gen. 33:18–19), and he dug a well there. The well, situated to the east of the ancient city mound and at the foot of "this mountain" (Mount Gerizim, John 4:20), is therefore the same well mentioned by John. By Jesus' day, it had already been used for a millennium. The toponym Sychar is either a corruption of the ancient name Shechem, or else it was another village a short distance away, at the ruins of what Arabs call Khirbet Askar.

The account continues that Jesus was wearied from the journey and sat down at the well. It was the sixth hour—twelve noon—the second day into his journey to Galilee, since Shechem is forty miles north of Jerusalem. Desiring to teach among the Samaritans, he had, in the first place, chosen this route to Galilee instead of the Jordan Valley route. Now in addition, he sent the Twelve to buy food for thirteen—again so he could have opportunity to strike up a conversation with a Samaritan, knowing that his friends might have spoiled the opportunity since "the Jews have no dealings with Samaritans." (John 4:9.)

For centuries, the Jews and Samaritans had drawn water from cisterns—underground water storage chambers—and from wells—like Jacob's Well. Jesus now told a Samaritan woman about the source of "living water," that is, ever-flowing or perennial water. Just as he intimated at the foot of Mount Hermon that he was the Rock of Salvation, and at Capernaum where mills were produced that he was the Bread of Life, so now at Jacob's Well he described himself as the Living Water, a source from which any person could draw spiritual water and quench spiritual thirst: "The water that I shall give him shall be in him a well of water springing up into everlasting life." (John 4:14.)

## INDIVIDUAL SITES IN JUDAEA

*Note: for Jerusalem, see chapter 12*

*Ephraim (see map, page 15, for location of this and all the following settlements)*

"[Jesus] went thence unto a country near to the wilderness, into a city called Ephraim." (John 11:54.) Following the raising of Lazarus in Bethany, Jesus found that walking openly among the Jews was dangerous. To escape the treacherous plans of some religious leaders, Jesus journeyed about fifteen miles northeast of Jerusalem out of the tribal inheritance of Judah and into the land of Ephraim (though still in the Roman province of Judaea during Jesus' day) to a small town known by the same name, Ephraim. The place had been called Ophrah in the Old Testament (see Josh. 18:23; 1 Sam. 13:17) and Apherema (cognate with Ephraim) in the Hasmonaean period (1 Maccabees 11:34). Today the Arab village of et-Taiyibe features several ancient and modern Christian churches that many of the Arab Christian villagers attend. There, "near to the wil-

derness," Jesus found respite before the final journey to Jerusalem.

*Ramah*

"In Rama was there a voice heard, lamentation, and weeping." (Matt. 2:18.) In connection with Herod's extermination order to kill all babies two years and under, Matthew cites a prophecy from Jeremiah 31:15 that there would be great lamentation and mourning in Rama(h), "Rachel weeping for her children, and would not be comforted, because they are not." (Matt. 2:16–18.)

Numerous Old Testament references and geographical notes of Josephus and early Church Fathers all fix the site of Ramah as five miles north of Jerusalem, in the land of Benjamin, along the trunk road leading to Samaria and Galilee. The present-day Arab village of er-Ram preserves the ancient name in Arabic. If Herod's edict involved the slaughter of infants in the environs of Bethlehem, which is five miles south of Jerusalem, what is the point then of the unrestrained mourning at Ramah, five miles north of Jerusalem?

The context of Jeremiah's prophecy is clearly the period of the Babylonian captivity. After Jeremiah's forty years of warning the inhabitants of Judah, he described the pathetic picture of Judaeans being carried away captive from the Babylonian military government position at Ramah: "The word that came to Jeremiah from the Lord, after that Nebuzaradan the captain of the guard had let him go from Ramah, when he had taken him being bound in chains among all that were carried away captive of Jerusalem and Judah,

30

which were carried away captive unto Babylon." (Jer. 40:1.) The Lord encouraged Jeremiah to "refrain [his] voice from weeping, and [his] eyes from tears: for . . . they shall come again from the land of the enemy. . . . Thy children shall come again to their own border." (Jer. 31:16–17.)

In commenting on the passage about Ramah, Edward Robinson wrote: "Eusebius and Jerome assume a Ramah near Bethlehem, in order to afford an explanation of the language of Matthew. This, however, is quite unnecessary. In the original passage of Jeremiah, Rachel, the ancestress of the tribe of Benjamin, is poetically introduced as bewailing the departure of her descendants into exile, from Ramah of Benjamin, their place of rendezvous."[2]

Matthew, who made constant reference to former-day prophecies that he saw fulfilled in the life and labors of Jesus, extracted this poetic picture of Jeremiah and accommodated the sense of it to a new event or circumstance. This may appear to be a form of falsification or text tampering to the modern mind uninitiated in Hebrew writing style and figures of speech, but this is an acceptable and typical Semitic literary device.

There are hundreds of cases where New Testament authors saw fulfillment of Old Testament passages in the words and works of Jesus. Matthew alone makes reference to nearly ninety passages from ten Old Testament books. Many things in the Old Testament are regarded as types of things to come. Following is another example of this use of typology, or what we could otherwise call multiple adaptation or multiple fulfillment of prophecy:

"When Israel was a child, then I loved him, and called my son out of Egypt." (Hosea 11:1.) Besides its application to the Israelite exodus from Egypt, Matthew adapts the verse to a new sense: Joseph "took the young child and his mother by night, and departed into Egypt: and was there until the death of Herod: that it might be fulfilled which was spoken of the Lord by the prophet, saying, Out of Egypt have I called my son." (2:14–15.)

### Arimathaea

"He was of Arimathaea, a city of the Jews." (Luke 23:51.) All four Gospel writers mention a man named Joseph who petitioned the Roman governor Pilate for Jesus' body to give it a proper burial. Matthew tells us that he was a rich man (see 27:57), and Luke describes him as "a good man, and a just" (23:50). Mark relates that he was an "honourable counsellor," meaning a member of the Sanhedrin (15:43), while Luke added that he had "not consented to the counsel and deed" of the other Sanhedrin members (see 23:51). John describes him as "a disciple of Jesus, but secretly for fear of the Jews." (19:38.)

Arimathaea is a Greek form of the Hebrew Ramah, or Ramot, or perhaps the dual form Ramathaim. Manuscript variants of these names include Armatha, Aramathoni, Armathaim, Ramatha, and Ramathem. Eusebius was first to associate Arimathaea with Rentis, in the district of Diospolis-Lod.[3] Josephus and 1 Maccabees both suggest a location to the east of Lod (Lydda). Rentis is located in the north-

31

western hills of Judaea (in the New Testament period), about thirty miles via Roman roads from Jerusalem.

## Bethlehem

"The city of David, which is called Bethlehem . . . " (Luke 2:4.) "Bethlehem of Judaea" is the usual rendering, to distinguish it from a Bethlehem in Galilee, just west of Nazareth in the territory of Zebulun. (See Josh. 19:10, 15.) Though Bethlehem figures in few biblical stories, yet the name is immortalized as the birthplace of two outstanding personalities in world history, King David and his descendant, Jesus Christ.

The prophetic word had gone forth centuries before (recorded at least by Micah) that the Messiah would be born a "son of David" in Bethlehem: "Thou, Beth-lehem Ephratah, though thou be little among the thousands of Judah, yet out of thee shall he come forth unto me that is to be ruler in Israel." (Micah 5:2.)

Matthew, of course, takes up Micah's prophecy to lend scriptural credibility to the divine and messianic origins of Jesus. In the citation of Micah, Matthew adds (apparently from 2 Sam. 5:2) "out of thee shall come a Governor [Greek, *leader*] that shall rule my people Israel" (Matt. 2:6). The Greek verb translated "rule" in this passage means to shepherd, tend, protect, or nurture.

In Matthew's account, "the chief priests and scribes of the people" (2:4) summoned by Herod are the ones who advised the king where Christ was to be born. It was generally known that the otherwise insignificant little Judaean town in this Roman period would perpetuate the glory of the Davidic dynasty by serving as birthplace of the Messiah. "Hath not the scripture said, That Christ cometh of the seed of David, and out of the town of Bethlehem, where David was?" (John 7:42.)

Matthew also records that Herod issued his infamous extermination order that infants under the age of two in the vicinity of Bethlehem be slaughtered so that he would have no contender to his throne. Herod "sent forth, and slew all the children that were in Bethlehem, and in all the coasts thereof, from two years old and under, according to the time which he had diligently enquired of the wise men." (Matt. 2:16.)

After the birth and infancy of Jesus in Bethlehem, we can find no further narrative mention in the New Testament of the town.

## Bethany and Bethphage

"Now Bethany was nigh unto Jerusalem, about fifteen furlongs off." (John 11:18.) When Jesus came to Jerusalem, he usually stayed in Bethany, situated about two miles east of Jerusalem on the eastern side of the Mount of Olives range. The fifteen furlongs, or stadia, is approximately two miles.

Bethany is likely the same as Ananiah of the Old Testament (see Neh. 11:32), though the names have different meanings (Ananiah signifying Jehovah covers—as a cloud does—and Bethany allegedly meaning house of dates). Today, the name of the town is el-Azariyeh, preserving the name of Lazarus, its famous former citizen. Jesus lodged with his friend Lazarus and his two sisters, Mary and Martha (see John 11:1), or with "Simon the leper," a man named Simon who had been a leper but was healed (see Matt. 26:6). The traditional tomb of Lazarus that visitors see today may be the tomb from which Jesus' dead friend was raised, though today's entrance is much higher than the original entryway.

"They drew nigh unto Jerusalem, and were come to Bethphage." (Matt. 21:1.) Two of the three passages referring to Bethphage mention it side by side with Bethany—the two towns were adjacent to each other, both on the eastern slope of the Mount of Olives. Bethphage means house of figs, and there are many fig trees growing in the vicinity.

Rabbinic literature cites Bethphage as the eastern limit to the city of Jerusalem.[4] Jesus' first coming to Jerusalem as king was from the east, as his second coming is prophesied to be. At Passover time, a time of independence, of victory over oppressors, of messianic expectation, Jesus accepted the acclamation of king and triumphantly proceeded into the city. (See Matt. 21.) He likely entered the Temple Mount where today's Golden Gate is located, and he turned into the temple, instead of into the Antonia Fortress to take on the Romans. That made all the difference—it showed what kind of Messiah he was.

## Emmaus

"A village called Emmaus, which was from Jerusalem about threescore furlongs . . . " (Luke 24:13.) Only Luke narrates a post-resurrection appearance of Jesus to two disciples walking along the road from Jerusalem down to Emmaus. There are three possible locations of this Judaean village: Emmaus Colonia, about three and a half miles northwest of Jerusalem; Qubeiba, about three miles northwest of Colonia; and Emmaus Nicopolis, about twenty miles northwest of Jerusalem at the edge of the Aijalon Valley.

Threescore furlongs, or sixty stadia, is what the verse says, though some early manuscripts indicate the distance was one hundred sixty stadia. If the latter figure is correct, then Emmaus Nicopolis could be the site intended, and it is the only one of the three candidates attested in historical records: many references to it are preserved through apocryphal writings and the works of Josephus Flavius during the Hellenistic-Roman periods.

On the other hand, twenty miles is far for the two disciples to walk to Emmaus and return to Jerusalem all in one evening. Already that memorable day had been full of events: Early in the morning, women had discovered that Jesus' tomb was empty and had circulated the shocking news. Other disciples had gone to verify the report. Later these two disciples had begun their walk to Emmaus and had encountered Jesus along the way, who apparently talked with them at length: "Beginning at Moses and all the prophets, he expounded unto them in all the scriptures the things concerning himself." (Luke 24:27.)

They approached the village at evening when the "day [was] far spent." (V. 29.) They prepared a meal and sat down to eat, and as he broke bread, they recognized who he was, and they "rose up the same hour, and returned to Jerusalem, and found the eleven gathered together, and them that were with them." (V. 33.)

With the day "far spent," it is unlikely that the disciples, as excited as they would have been, would rush out the door to begin a twenty-mile, six- to seven-hour return trip up to Jerusalem and at the end of the journey still find disciples gathered in a meeting. A more likely candidate for New Testament Emmaus may be Emmaus Colonia, situated one to two hours' walking distance west of Jerusalem, at today's suburb of Motza.

## INDIVIDUAL SITES IN THE RIFT VALLEY AND THE FAR SOUTH

*Aenon and Salim (see map, page 15, for location of this and all the following settlements)*

"John also was baptizing in Aenon near to Salim, because there was much water there." (John 3:23.) We have three possibilities for the place where John was baptizing:

1. The sixth-century Medeba Map, an east-oriented, mosaic map that is our oldest cartographic representation of the Holy Land, shows Aenon on the eastern side of the Jordan River opposite Jericho, near Bethabara where John was baptizing. (See John 1:28.)

2. Eusebius preserved a tradition of Aenon, being about seven miles south of Beth-shan.[5] There is nearby a site called Salem, now Tel Shalem.

3. Still another possible location for

Aenon was near Neapolis—modern Nablus, or ancient Shechem—not far from where Eusebius noted that another Salim/Salem was located.[6] (Cf. Gen. 33:18.) Aenon means springs in Hebrew, and there are many of them around that country. The Aenon might have been the prolific springs at Tel Far'ah. Another connection with John the Baptist in the hills of Samaria is the Crusader "Church of the Invention of the Head of St. John the Baptist" at the ruins of ancient Samaria.

There seems to be no way at present to identify with certainty which of the three sites is alluded to in the passage, but it does appear possible that John baptized in more than one location in the land of the Jews. Ascertaining the location of John's baptismal site would be easier if we had sure answers to several questions about the verse from John. The previous verse (John 3:22) mentions that Jesus and his disciples were baptizing (see also JST, John 4:1–4). Then verse twenty-three indicates that John also was baptizing.

Could the one verse simply serve as a parallel to the other? Does the "also" in verse twenty-three mean that John was baptizing there in addition to others baptizing, or that he was baptizing there in addition to his Peraea site? And why is the quantity of water at the site particularly mentioned? Is it simply because the Jordan Valley has plenty of water for immersing people completely in water, which is the Jewish way of baptizing? Or is the Gospel writer making a point that John was also baptizing in a place where there was "much water" because they were away from the usual immersion

34

*Top left:* Modern Bethlehem, as seen from Shepherds' Fields. *Top right:* Baptizing in the Jordan River. *Center left:* Site of Roman-period Jericho (immediately above the hikers' heads), with the oasis of modern-day Jericho in the background. *Center right:* Unexcavated fortress of Machaerus, possible site of John the Baptist's death. *Bottom left:* Port of Acco, known in New Testament times as Ptolemais. *Bottom right:* Inscription mentioning Tiberius and Pontius Pilate, found in the ruins of the theater of Caesarea.

places? Maybe "because there was much water there" suggests an inland site.

## Jericho

"Jesus entered and passed through Jericho." (Luke 19:1.) Old Testament Jericho (Tel es-Sultan), conquered and destroyed by Joshua and abandoned through most of the Israelite period, had lain in ruins for many centuries by Jesus' day. Hasmonaean kings had begun a new Jericho along the north bank of Wadi Kelt, over a mile south of the former site of Jericho. Herod the Great spread magnificent palaces, pavilions, a bathhouse, a swimming pool, a reception hall, and gardens along both banks of the wadi. It was an inviting oasis surrounded by stark wilderness, with the Dead Sea just five miles away.

Hasmonaean-Roman period Jericho served as a rest station for weary travelers coming from Galilee to Judaea (see Matt. 20:29; Luke 19:1) and as an entry point at the border between Peraea and Judaea. Zacchaeus was a chief tax collector in Jericho, and he was rich. (See Luke 19:2.) He was apparently a sincere and honest man (see 19:8) who was small of stature, for when he heard that Jesus was approaching, he climbed a sycomore tree to see him. Jesus invited him down so the publican could host him at his home. On another occasion, when Jesus left Jericho with a great number of people accompanying him, about to begin the hike up the Roman road to Jerusalem through the Judaean Desert, he stopped and healed a blind man named Bartimaeus. (See Mark 10:46–52.)

The most famous reference to Jericho in the New Testament is the beginning line of the parable of the good Samaritan: "A certain man went down from Jerusalem to Jericho, and fell among thieves." (Luke 10:30.) Though a fictional story, the parable was true to the social and historical setting of the day. The story makes reference to Levites and priests along the Jericho Road, and excavators at Roman period Jericho have uncovered many houses belonging to priests who could have worked in the Jerusalem Temple. "Jericho, the garden city, which during the days of the Second Temple extended over thousands of dunams and was inhabited by tens of thousands of Jews, many of them priests, probably shrank after 70 C.E."[7]

## Bethabara

"These things were done in Bethabara beyond Jordan, where John was baptizing." (John 1:28.) As we have seen, "beyond Jordan" is the name of a region on the east bank of the Jordan River (Greek, *Peraea*). The toponym *Bethabara* appears in most manuscripts (as in the King James Version, and as the church father Origen of Caesarea preferred), while *Bethany* appears in others (as in the Revised Standard Version). We have no other literary or archaeological evidence of a Bethany near the Jordan River opposite Jericho.

There is actually no problem with having two Bethanys in eastern Judaea—the Bible has numerous examples of repetitive use of place names: there were several towns named Ramah, Gibeah, Gath, Carmel, Mizpeh, Aroer, and Socoh, for instance. Yet we hold that Bethabara was the correct name of the site of John's baptizing. Nephi recorded a prophecy from his father Lehi that John would "baptize in Bethabara, beyond Jordan." (1 Ne. 10:9.) Bethabara appears on the Medeba Map at the natural fording place east of Jericho entering Peraea. In Hebrew, Bethabara or Beth-avara means place of crossing. At such an important juncture along a major east-west travel route, John could have taught all the souls coming from the regions of Judaea, Peraea, Galilee, Decapolis, and Phoenicia.

"They came unto John, and said unto him, Rabbi, he that was with thee beyond Jordan, to whom thou barest witness, behold, the same baptizeth, and all men come to him." (John 3:26.) Just across the Jordan opposite Jericho is where the closing scenes of the ministries of the great prophets Moses and Elijah occurred—an appropriate location for the opening scenes of the ministries of the great Forerunner and the Messiah.

## Machaerus

"Herod had laid hold on John, and bound him, and put him in prison." (Matt. 14:3.) John the Baptist had been preaching in Peraea in the tetrarchy of Herod Antipas, and he had denounced Antipas's adulterous and incestuous relationship with Herodias, his half-brother Philip's former wife. Herodias was responsible for John's arrest. The New Testament itself cites no specific place for the imprisonment and execution of the Baptist. We can only trust the accuracy of the historical report of Josephus, who wrote, "John, because of Herod's suspicions, was brought in chains to Machaerus . . . and put to death."[8]

Machaerus sits at the edge of the Transjordanian Mountains overlooking the Dead Sea, near the southern border of Peraea. The Hasmonaean King Alexander Jannaeus had reared the fortress, but the earliest Roman forces destroyed it. Herod the Great rebuilt it, along with Masada on the other side of the Dead Sea. There, in that forlorn corner of desolation, and beneath the pomp and revelry in the palace where Antipas and Herodias had traveled to celebrate Antipas's birthday, the blade of the executioner released John from his mortal labors.

## Sodom and Gomorrah

"It shall be more tolerable for Sodom and Gomorrha in the day of judgment, than for that city." (Mark 6:11.) Sodom and Gomorrah, like Tyre and Sidon, are a toponymic pair—their names almost always occur together in geographic references. Throughout biblical writings, the cities of Sodom and Gomorrah epitomized the most despicable living conditions. In the New Testament, Sodom and Gomorrah are always mentioned in connection with cursing, evil living, and destruction. Because of their iniquities, the Lord "rained fire and brimstone from heaven, and destroyed them all." (Luke 17:29.) The sin centers of Sodom and Gomorrah were physically situated at the lowest point on earth, and the moral behavior of their inhabitants is typically described as the lowest and most degrading on earth.

When condemning his own town Capernaum, Jesus intensified the curse by comparing it with Sodom. (See Matt.

11:23–24.) Had the depraved people of Sodom heard and seen the same teachings and miracles as the people of Capernaum heard and saw, they would have repented sufficiently to avert the doom and destruction that engulfed them. It would be less tolerable for the people of Capernaum in the day of judgment because they had greater witness of divine things, yet the majority still rejected Jesus.

Peter later commented on the fate of Sodom and Gomorrah: "Turning the cities of Sodom and Gomorrha into ashes condemned them with an overthrow, making them an ensample unto those that after should live ungodly." (2 Pet. 2:6.) The word *overthrow* (the Greek word has come directly into English as *catastrophe*) is used frequently in the Old Testament also. In every case that the Hebrew word (*mahapekha*) is used, it refers to Sodom and Gomorrah and suggests an earthquake. The cities were located at the southern end of the Dead Sea, in the Rift Valley, one of the longest and deepest cracks in the earth's surface, an earthquake fault-zone. The overthrowing or overturning of Sodom and Gomorrah could have been caused by, or at least accompanied by, an earthquake.

Jude added another dimension to the destructive process: "Even as Sodom and Gomorrha, and the cities about them in like manner, giving themselves over to fornication, and going after strange flesh, are set forth for an example, suffering the vengeance of eternal fire." (Jude 1:7.) He labeled the destroying agent as "eternal fire," possibly some radiance or energy from the Divine Power. (Cf. Gen. 19:24;

Ex. 3:2; 13:21; and especially Lev. 10:2; Num. 16:35—"fire from the Lord" that consumed others.)

## Mount Sinai and the Red Sea

For the sake of completeness, we should note that in the New Testament there are four references by name and one by the word "mount" to Mount Sinai. (See Acts 7:30, 38; Gal. 4:24–25; Heb. 8:5.) There are also two references to the Red Sea. (See Acts 7:36; Heb. 11:29.) All these references are used in the context of historical reminders of the Lord's dealings with the Israelites during the Exodus from Egypt and during the wilderness wanderings.

## INDIVIDUAL SITES IN THE COASTAL PLAINS

In looking at the involvement of coastal cities in the New Testament record, we must shift our attention to apostles and missionaries in the early Christian Church. All references to the following seven cities occur beginning in the Acts of the Apostles. Except for a visit to "the coasts of Tyre and Sidon" (Matt. 15:21–28; Mark 7:24–31), we have no record of Jesus ever laboring along the gentile coast. His one recorded visit may have been prompted by the presence of Tyrians and Sidonians while he taught and healed in Galilee: "They about Tyre and Sidon, a great multitude, when they had heard what great things he did, came unto him." (Mark 3:8.) "From the sea coast of Tyre and Sidon . . . [they] came to hear him, and to be healed of their diseases." (Luke 6:17.)

*Ptolemais (see map, page 15, for location of this and all the following settlements)*

"When we had finished our course from Tyre, we came to Ptolemais." (Acts 21:7.) The great ancient port city of Acco is mentioned only once in the New Testament by its Hellenistic-Roman period name, Ptolemais. It was the main natural port city of the Holy Land, situated across the bay (north) from modern Haifa. On his third missionary journey, en route to Jerusalem, Paul stopped to visit those in Ptolemais who had earlier adopted Christianity.

## Caesarea

In honor of Caesar Augustus, Herod the Great built a magnificent port city halfway between Ptolemais and Joppa along the sand-duned coast two decades before Jesus. The eight-thousand-acre site is now under intensive excavation, revealing the pomp and splendor of the grandest builder the Holy Land has ever known. Aqueduct, hippodrome, colonnaded mosaic cardo, theater, brick drainage and sewerage system, and port facility, in addition to palaces, temples, and other public structures, are all being uncovered in one of the Roman world's truly impressive cities.

Four names deserve special mention in New Testament Caesarea, all from Acts: Philip, Peter, Cornelius, and Paul. Philip was one of seven men "of honest report, full of the Holy Ghost and wisdom" (Acts 6:3) appointed as assistants to the twelve apostles to take care of the Church's temporal affairs. He taught, baptized, and performed miracles among the people of Samaria, Gaza, Azotus, and other coastal cities. Then we find him residing in Caesarea with his four unmarried prophetess daughters. (See Acts 8:40; 21:8–9.) At the end of Paul's mission, he and his company stayed with Philip's family in Caesarea for a time. (See Acts 21:9–10.)

Caesarea was involved in the dramatic opening of the gospel to the Gentiles. Peter, the president of the Church, was at Jewish Joppa (see further on Joppa), thirty-four miles south of Caesarea. He and an Italian centurion named Cornelius stationed in Caesarea were having simultaneous visionary experiences that would lead to proselyting Romans, Greeks, and others. Cornelius is the first known Gentile (excluding Samaritans) to receive the gospel without first being a Jew.

Between A.D. 41 and 44, Jews experienced something of a "golden era" under Herod Agrippa I, having for those few years a Herodian leader instead of a Roman governor. It was not, however, a golden era for Christians. At Passover time in Jerusalem, Agrippa apprehended and executed James, one of the presidency of the Church, "and because he saw it pleased the Jews, he proceeded further to take Peter also." (Acts 12:2–3.) By divine intervention Peter managed to escape, and Agrippa "went down from Judaea to Caesarea, and there abode." (Acts 12:19.)

Sometime later, while apparently celebrating Rome's victory over Britain, Agrippa arrived in Caesarea's theater wearing a solid silver robe, gave an ostentatious oration, and was acclaimed a god by his constituents. "Immediately the angel of the Lord smote him, because he gave not God the glory: and he was eaten of worms." (Acts 12:21–23.)

Paul, in and out of Caesarea on his missions (see Acts 18:22; 21:8), was eventually arraigned before Roman procurators Felix and Festus and before a visiting king, Herod Agrippa II (see Acts 24–26). Finding no hope of justice from Jews pressing their cause against him in Caesarea, Paul appealed to Nero and sailed for Rome.

### Antipatris

"Then the soldiers . . . took Paul, and brought him by night to Antipatris." (Acts 23:31.) Because of Jewish threats to kill Paul, he was escorted by 470 soldiers, horsemen, and spearmen, leaving Jerusalem at the third hour of the night. (See Acts 23:23.) En route to Caesarea, Paul and his bodyguard stopped temporarily at Antipatris.

The Old Testament name of this site was Aphek. The Israelites and Philistines fought several critical battles near Aphek, a city shown by recent excavations to have been of great importance for many centuries. Ramses II's governor of Canaan owned a palace at Aphek, and Herod the Great later built a fortress and city there.

The geographical importance of Aphek/Antipatris, not only to Israelites, but also to the entire Near East, lies in its position along the International Highway (Via Maris). The city was situated at the springs that immediately became the Yarkon River, which flows out toward the Mediterranean Sea. (Today some of the Yarkon spring waters are pumped up to

Jerusalem and all the way south to the Negev.) All traffic, local and international, was channeled into the mile-wide corridor between the springs and the hills. Geographical factors had thus given strategic value to the site, so Herod took advantage of it and established a city named for his father, Antipater.

### Lydda

"He came down also to the saints which dwelt at Lydda." (Acts 9:32.) Old Testament Lod, otherwise known as Lydda in the New Testament record, is one of the towns visited by Peter on his tour of the missions. It is situated along the main road from Jerusalem to Joppa. There had already been some teaching activity by the apostles and the seventy in the coastal towns, particularly since the Resurrection, so Peter "passed throughout all quarters" (Acts 9:32), giving further instructions to the various congregations of saints. A man named Aeneas, who had been paralyzed for eight years, was healed, "and all that dwelt at Lydda and Saron saw him, and turned to the Lord." (Acts 9:33–35.)

### Joppa

"Forasmuch as Lydda was nigh to Joppa, and the disciples had heard that Peter was there, they sent . . . desiring him that he would not delay to come to them." (Acts 9:38.) A woman disciple named Tabitha (an Aramaic name meaning gazelle; in Greek, Dorcas) had died, and the whole community of saints was in deep mourning, showing her handiwork and remembering her good works.

Peter arrived and ushered them out of the chamber. Then he prayed and proceeded to do what he had seen Jesus do: he raised her from the dead. "And it was known throughout all Joppa; and many believed in the Lord." (Acts 9:42.)

Peter stayed quite some time in Joppa, Jerusalem's port city, lodging in the seaside house of a tanner named Simon (another of the nine Simons in the New Testament). While the prophet-president resided at Joppa, the great vision was opened to him that the gospel should go also to the Gentiles. (See Acts 10.) Cornelius, the Roman army officer in Caesarea, had received divine instruction to contact Simon Peter. Peter had gone up to pray on the housetop about the sixth hour—noontime—and he became very hungry. Inclined to get up and go for food, he fell into a trance; that is, he was completely overshadowed by the Spirit of God—and was advised three times in a unique vision to rise up and eat what God had prepared for him.

The meaning of the vision began unfolding with a knock at the gate of Simon's house. Peter agreed to follow the emissaries of Cornelius back to Caesarea, a distance of thirty-four miles, approximately eleven hours of walking. Cornelius and his household subsequently converted to the gospel, and they experienced an outpouring of the Holy Ghost. With the conversion of an Italian family, the history of the Church would never be the same again; a bold and dramatic thrust into the pagan world signaled a wider vision of the meaning and purpose of the Church Jesus had established in Galilee and Judaea.

## Azotus and Gaza

"Philip was found at Azotus." (Acts 8:40.) The name of Old Testament Ashdod, one of the five major cities of the Philistines, was changed in Hellenistic times to Azotus. It was the scene of some of Philip's missionary activity among hellenized Jews, Greeks, and Romans residing there.

"The angel of the Lord spake unto Philip, saying, Arise, and go toward the south unto the way that goeth down from Jerusalem unto Gaza, which is desert." (Acts 8:26.) The angelic instruction to Philip included specific mention of a highway. Philip was told to exit Jerusalem going south until he came to the turn-off of the Jerusalem-Gaza Road, likely the Roman road along the Bether ridge down into the Elah Valley (remnants of which still exist), then through the Shephelah past Beth Guvrin and southwest to the international highway and on to Gaza.

Philip was told to journey along that particular road so as to meet a eunuch or officer of the court of Candace, queen of the Ethiopians (*Candace* is a Meroitic or Cushite name-title for queen—as are *pharaoh* for Egyptian kings and *Caesar* for Roman emperors.) This court official, being deeply religious, had come to Jerusalem to worship. He was versed in the Hebrew scriptures, but while reading Isaiah (chapter 53), Philip stopped him and asked if he needed help interpreting the passage. Philip taught him about Jesus, and the Ethiopian desired baptism. When they came to a body of water deep enough for immersion, "they went down both into the water, both Philip and the eunuch; and he baptized him." (Acts 8:38.) The account refers to the Jerusalem-Gaza way, "which is desert"; that is, the highway from the hill country southwest toward the desert (northern Sinai), which begins at Gaza.

## NOTES

1. *Biblical Researches in Palestine,* 4 vols. (Boston: Crocker & Brewster, 1841 and 1856), 2:628.

2. *Biblical Researches,* 4:273.

3. *Onomastikon,* 144:27–29.

4. See Herbert Danby, tr., *The Mishnah* (London: Oxford University Press, 1933), 500 n. 11.

5. *Onomastikon,* 40:1.

6. *Onomastikon,* 160:13.

7. Ehud Netzer, *Bulletin of the American Schools of Oriental Research,* 228 (1977): 12.

8. Josephus, *Antiquities,* tr. Louis Feldman (Cambridge: Harvard University Press, 1965), XVIII.119.

# SURROUNDING NATIONS

*"Unto the uttermost part of the earth . . . " (Acts 1:8.)*

What were the geographical perimeters of the world in a typical Judaean's mind in the days of Jesus? What was the reach of his geographical knowledge? The early Christians received a commission to be witnesses of Jesus not only in Jerusalem, Judaea, and Samaria, but also "unto the uttermost part of the earth." (Acts 1:8.) What would the "uttermost part of the earth" have meant to those Jewish Christians?

That phrase does appear in another context in the Gospels. Referring to the Queen of Sheba, Matthew and Luke indicate that "she came from the uttermost parts of the earth to hear the wisdom of Solomon." (Matt. 12:42; Luke 11:31.) The land of Sheba or Seba—the land of the Sabaeans—was the southwestern part of today's Arabian Peninsula, specifically the modern land of Yemen. Was that the "uttermost part of the earth" to the Jews?

The Hellenistic-Roman world was as open and trafficable as the world had ever been. Land and sea routes crisscrossed each other in myriad directions; economic enterprises spanned the Empire. Great centers of learning dotted the Mediterranean lands. The Jews had made a particular mark on nations and societies everywhere. Diaspora communities still had great ties to the homeland, and Jerusalem wielded unique influence throughout the Empire. Strabo, a Greek historian and geographer writing in the first century A.D., indicated that Jews had made their way "into every city, and it is not easy to find any place in the habitable world which has not received this nation and in which it has not made its power felt."[1]

Philo, an Alexandrian philosopher and contemporary with Jesus, in issuing a veiled threat to Caligula (who wanted to set up his own statue in Jerusalem), wrote that the holy city of Jerusalem was "the mother city not of one country Judaea but of most of the others in virtue of the colonies sent out at diverse times to the neighbouring lands Egypt, Phoenicia, the part of Syria called Hollow [Coele-Syria; that is, the Lebanese Beq'a] . . . and lying far apart, Pamphylia, Cilicia, most of Asia [Minor] up to Bithynia and the corners of Pontus, similarly also into Europe, Thessaly, Boeotia, Macedonia, Aetolia, Attica, Argos, Corinth and most of the best parts of Peloponnese. And not only are the mainlands full of Jewish colonies but also the most highly esteemed of the islands Euboea, Cyprus, Crete. I say nothing of the countries beyond the Euphrates. . . . So that if my own home city is granted a share of your goodwill the benefit extends not to one city but to myriads of the others situated in every region of the inhabited world."[2]

Jews throughout the Empire looked to Jerusalem for calendar and legalistic questions. They sent money to Jerusalem from all parts of the Empire for the upkeep of the Temple and the Holy City.

Judaeans living in the time of Jesus likely had a wider compass of geographical knowledge than people in any previous era. In his own native land, the typical Judaean could have heard four different languages being used. He himself would have known Aramaic and Hebrew, and he might have had daily contact with those speaking Greek and Latin. So that all could read it, the superscription on Jesus' cross was "written in Hebrew, and Greek, and Latin." (John 19:20.)

## The Day of Pentecost

At least yearly, Judaeans would expect to see fellow Jews and other curious tourists and travelers from all parts of the Roman world. Jerusalem was an international city. One of the most comprehensive lists of place names in the Bible recites the origin of those attending the Shavuot Festival, the day of Pentecost, shortly after Jesus' departure into heaven. Luke accurately reported that there were present: "Jews, devout men, out of every nation under heaven . . . Parthians, and Medes, and Elamites, and the dwellers in Mesopotamia, and in Judaea, and Cappadocia, in Pontus, and Asia, Phrygia, and Pamphylia, in Egypt, and in the parts of Libya about Cyrene, and strangers of Rome, Jews and proselytes, Cretes and Arabians." (Acts 2:5, 9–11.)

Following is a list of those geographical regions with modern equivalents (see map on page 45):

| Ancient Name | Modern Equivalent |
| --- | --- |
| EAST: | |
| Parthia | eastern Iran |
| Media | western Iran |
| Elam | southwest Iran |
| Mesopotamia | Iraq |
| NORTH: | |
| Pontus | northern Turkey |
| Cappadocia | central Turkey |
| Asia | western Turkey |
| Phrygia | west-central Turkey |
| Pamphylia | southern Turkey |
| SOUTH: | |
| Egypt | Egypt; NE Africa |
| Libya | coastal Africa west of Egypt |
| Cyrene | a chief city of Libya or Cyrenaica |
| Arabia | great desert lands south and east of Judaea |
| WEST: | |
| Crete | same as today; large island south of Greece |
| Rome | same as in Italy today |

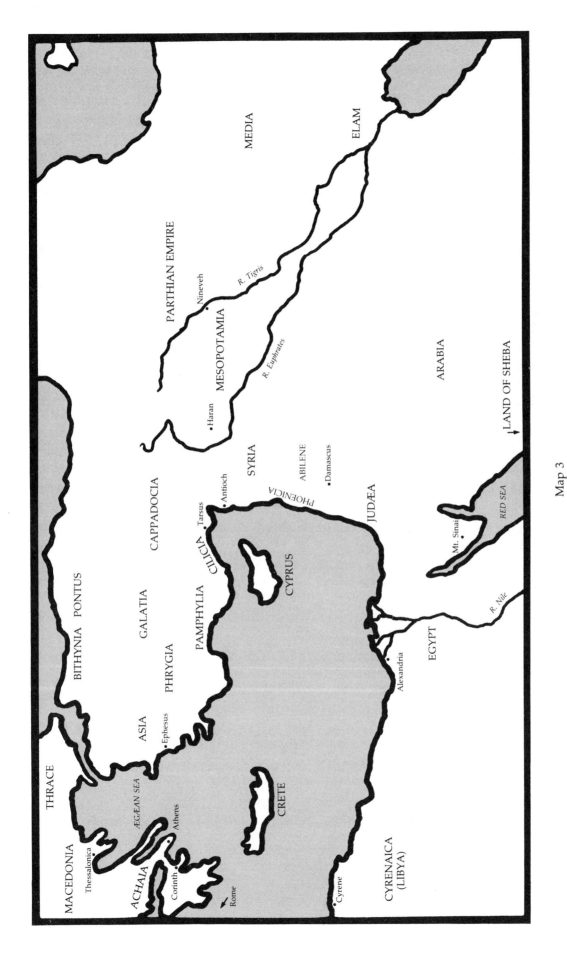

Map 3

The land of the Bible and surrounding regions.

Judaeans, then, would have had some acquaintance with Jews and non-Jews from a rather wide compass, from beyond Mesopotamia to Rome and from the borders of Europe to north Africa.

## NATIONS SURROUNDING THE HOLY LAND

### Egypt

The religious history of Israel is inextricably tied to the land of Egypt. The great patriarchs and prophets Abraham, Jacob, Joseph, Moses, and Jeremiah all spent part of their lives in the land of pyramids, tombs, and temples. Egypt played a significant role as a place of refuge—either economic or political refuge. Abraham and Jacob had both gone down into Egypt to escape famine (because of the ever-flowing Nile, the land of Egypt knew famine less often than other lands). Jeroboam and Joseph, with Mary and Jesus, fled there to escape political dangers.

In the early Roman period, hundreds of thousands of Jews lived in Egypt, particularly in Alexandria. Some made annual pilgrimages to Jerusalem for the great festivals, like Pentecost. (Acts 2:10.) Jews from Alexandria debated with Stephen, one of the officials of the Christian Church in Jerusalem. (See Acts 6:9.) Interestingly, most references to Egypt in the New Testament come from the speech on the religious history of the Hebrew people that Stephen gave to his antagonists—ten occurrences in Acts 7.

### Cyrenaica

The reference in Acts concerning the day of Pentecost is the only one mention-

ing the widespread nations until the accounts of Paul's journeys, with the exception of Cyrene. The New Testament contains a surprising number of allusions to Cyrenian Jews and Christians: "As they led him away, they laid hold upon one Simon, a Cyrenian, coming out of the country, and on him they laid the cross, that he might bear it after Jesus." (Luke 23:26.)

Cyrene was a Mediterranean port on the northern coast of Africa and the chief city of the Roman province Cyrenaica (or western Libya). Though in Africa, Cyrene had been settled as a Greek city, and by Jesus' day it had a large colony of Jews.

Many Cyrenians took an active stance either for or against the young Christian message. "Then there arose certain of the synagogue, which is called the synagogue of the Libertines, and Cyrenians, and Alexandrians, and of them of Cilicia and of Asia, disputing with Stephen." (Acts 6:9.) "Some of them were men of Cyprus and Cyrene, which, when they were come to Antioch, spake unto the Grecians, preaching the Lord Jesus." (Acts 11:20.) "Now there were in the church that was at Antioch certain prophets and teachers; as Barnabas, and Simeon that was called Niger, and Lucius of Cyrene." (Acts 13:1.)

### Mesopotamia

In addition to the single reference about residents of Mesopotamia being present at Pentecost, Stephen's historical review also alluded to Abraham's Mesopotamian homeland: "Men, brethren, and fathers, hearken; The God of glory appeared unto our father Abraham,

Along the Nile River, where Joseph, Mary, and the infant Jesus lived for a time.

Haran, in Upper Mesopotamia, where Abraham lived before journeying to Canaan.

Modern Antakya, Turkey, ancient Antioch of Syria—great center of the early Church.

when he was in Mesopotamia, before he dwelt in Charran [Haran in Genesis]." (Acts 7:2.) "Then came he out of the land of the Chaldaeans, and dwelt in Charran: and from thence, when his father was dead, he removed him into this land, wherein ye now dwell." (Acts 7:4.)

The only other New Testament reference to a place in Mesopotamia is Jesus' mention of the preaching of Jonah to the people of Nineveh, thus confirming the historicity of the prophet and the incident: "The men of Nineveh shall rise in judgment with this generation, and shall condemn it: because they repented at the preaching of Jonas; and, behold, a greater than Jonas is here." (Matt. 12:41.)

## Syria-Phoenicia

One of the benefactors of Jesus' healing power was a Greek woman, specifically a gentile woman, "a Syrophenician by nation." (Mark 7:26.) In Jesus' day, Phoenicia, the coastal region with the old cities Sidon, Sarepta, and Tyre, was part of the Roman province of Syria: "[Paul and company] sailed into Syria, and landed at Tyre." (Acts 21:3.)

Sites in Phoenicia also figured in the spread of the early Christian Church: "Now they which were scattered abroad upon the persecution that arose about Stephen travelled as far as Phenice, . . . preaching the word to none but unto the Jews only." (Acts 11:19.) "Being brought on their way by the church, they passed through Phenice and Samaria, declaring the conversion of the Gentiles." (Acts 15:3.) We have already seen how multitudes of people journeyed from the area

around Tyre and Sidon to hear Jesus teach, and how Jesus himself visited the Tyrians and Sidonians in their cities. (See "Individual Sites in the Coastal Plain," chapter 2.)

Paul's missionary journeys later included stops at Tyre and Sidon: "[We] landed at Tyre: for there the ship was to unlade her burden. . . . And when we had finished our course from Tyre, we came to Ptolemais." (Acts 21:3, 7.) On Paul's voyage to Rome, Luke recorded the itinerary in some detail: "The next day we touched at Sidon. And Julius courteously entreated Paul, and gave him liberty to go unto his friends to refresh himself." (Acts 27:3.)

The first reference to Syria (Old Testament Aram) in the life of Jesus is the mention by Luke of one Cyrenius, who was the Roman governor of the province of Syria at the birth of Jesus. Though there is some uncertainty about the dating of the census, or enrollment, that Luke mentioned, yet the service of Roman consul P. Sulpicius Quirinius as governor (legate) of Syria during the initial years of the first millennium A.D. is confirmed also by the Jewish historian Josephus.

Just as the old prophets of Israel had used their curative priesthood powers on foreigners—"Many lepers were in Israel in the time of Eliseus [Elisha] the prophet; and none of them was cleansed, saving Naaman the Syrian" (Luke 4:27)—so in Jesus' early ministry, "his fame went throughout all Syria: and they brought unto him all sick people that were taken with divers diseases and torments, and those which were possessed with devils, and those which were lunatick, and those that had the palsy; and he healed them" (Matt. 4:24).

Luke wrote that the ministries of John and Jesus began when Pilate was governor of Judaea, Herod Antipas the tetrarch of Galilee, his brother Philip the tetrarch of Ituraea and Trachonitis, and "Lysanias the tetrarch of Abilene." (Luke 3:1.) Abilene was a region, named after its capital city Abila (not to be confused with Abila, a city of the Decapolis further south), which was situated about twenty miles northwest of Damascus. The governor of Abilene, Lysanias, is mentioned not only by Luke but on an inscription at Abila dating from the reign of Tiberius.

The historic city of Damascus is mentioned seven times with a fair amount of detail (including the name of one of its streets, "Straight," in Acts 9:11). All the references to Damascus are in Acts 9, in connection with the conversion of Saul to Christianity. The city had a large number of Jews, and Saul felt the need to go there and root out the Jewish Christians: "Saul, yet breathing out threatenings and slaughter against the disciples of the Lord, went unto the high priest, and desired of him letters to Damascus to the synagogues, that if he found any of this way, whether they were men or women, he might bring them bound unto Jerusalem." (Vv. 1–2.) Instead, after his conversion, Saul ended up testifying of Jesus in those very synagogues. He so angered the Jews that they plotted to kill him, and Saul escaped by being let down in a basket over the walls at night.

The greatest city in Syria in the days of Jesus was its capital in the northwest corner of the province called Antioch (modern Antakya in Turkey). After Rome and Alexandria, Antioch was the third largest city in the Roman Empire and one of its greatest cultural and commercial centers. Jews from this city three hundred miles north of Jerusalem were quite active in the religious life of the Holy City. One of the seven Greeks chosen as leaders in the early Christian Church was a Jewish convert who had become Christian, "Nicolas a proselyte of Antioch." (Acts 6:5).

Early persecution had caused some Christians to flee the Holy Land to other parts of the Empire. "They which were scattered abroad upon the persecution that arose about Stephen travelled as far as . . . Antioch, preaching the word to none but unto the Jews only." (Acts 11:19–20.) Antioch became pivotal in the growth of the Church. "They sent forth Barnabas, that he should go as far as Antioch. . . . When he had found [Paul], he brought him unto Antioch. And it came to pass, that a whole year they assembled themselves with the church, and taught much people. And the disciples were called Christians first in Antioch. And in these days came prophets from Jerusalem unto Antioch." (Acts 11:22, 26–27.)

*Asia*

The catalog of countries represented on the day of Pentecost includes Cappadocia, Pontus, and Asia. (See Acts 2:9.) The province referred to as "Asia" meant the westernmost region of modern Turkey, extending west to the Aegaean Sea. There were Jews of Asia disputing with

49

Stephen in Jerusalem (Acts 6:9), as well as "Jews which were of Asia" stirring up the people against Paul in the Temple (Acts 21:27; 24:18).

Another specific region mentioned frequently in Acts was Cilicia, the home province of Paul: "I am a man which am a Jew of Tarsus, a city in Cilicia, a citizen of no mean city." (Acts 21:39; see also 22:3; 23:34.) Paul labored among his own native Cilicians: "He went through Syria and Cilicia, confirming the churches." (Acts 15:41.)

## Cyprus

One of the early leaders of the Christian Church in Jerusalem was a diaspora Jew named Joseph, who was from Cyprus: "Joses, who by the apostles was surnamed Barnabas, (which is, being interpreted, The son of consolation,) a Levite, and of the country of Cyprus." (Acts 4:36.) Some of the Jewish Christians who fled the persecutions surrounding Stephen's martyrdom also traveled to Cyprus (see Acts 11:19), and some Christian Cypriots traveled to Antioch to preach about Jesus (Acts 11:20).

Another reference to the island is given in the story of Paul's last trip to Jerusalem: "Now when we had discovered Cyprus, we left it on the left hand [that is, to the north], and sailed into Syria, and landed at Tyre." (Acts 21:3.)

Having identified the neighboring countries of the Holy Land referred to in the Gospels and Acts, we can see that Judaeans living at the time of Jesus had a geographical perspective of the world that was broad indeed. They had contact with Jews and non-Jews from the states contiguous with Israel—that is, Syria (including Phoenicia and Transjordan), Arabia, and Egypt—from Mesopotamia and beyond, from Asia Minor and Greece, from Rome, from the islands of the Mediterranean, and from north Africa. The commission to take the gospel to the "uttermost parts of the earth" was an expansive challenge issued out of the humble hill country of Judaea.

### NOTES

1. Josephus, *Antiquities,* tr. Ralph Marcus, in Loeb Classical Library (Cambridge: Harvard University Press, 1971), XIV:115.

2. *The Embassy to Gaius,* tr. F. H. Colson, in *Philo,* vol. X, in Loeb Classical Library, 281–83.

# CHAPTER 4

# WATER RESOURCES AND USES

*"Whosoever drinketh of the water that I shall give him shall never thirst."* (*John 4:14.*)

There is a saying inscribed on signs near prolific springs in the mountainous terrain of modern Turkey, "From water comes all life." Water *is* life to citizens of the Near East, ancient and modern. Recent history has emphasized, even exaggerated, the importance of oil as a source of energy and as a political weapon, yet clearly the foremost issue in the Near East has always been, and still is, *water.*

The God of the Hebrews had warned his people that, living as they were at the edge of the great deserts, they would have to be faithful to his commandments to be assured of a continuous supply of life-sustaining water. They knew that rain came not from the clouds but from heaven. (See Lev. 26:3–4; Deut. 11:10–17.)

The New Testament reflects the prominence of water in the mentality of Jews in Jesus' day. Rewards of righteous discipleship are illustrated with the following promise: "Whosoever shall give to drink unto one of these little ones a cup of cold water . . . , he shall in no wise lose his reward." (Matt. 10:42; see Mark 9:41.)

The activities of Jesus in both Galilee and Judaea were not far from water. (See "Go, wash in the pool of Siloam," chapter 12, for water sources in Jerusalem.) Jesus was baptized in the Jordan River (see Matt. 3); he summoned some of his future apostles while they were fishing in the Sea of Galilee (see Matt. 4:18–22); he gave his Living Water sermon by Jacob's Well (see John 4); he healed a man at the Pool of Bethesda (see John 5), and he sent another man to be healed at the Pool of Siloam (see John 9).

Jesus also showed on more than one occasion his control of the elements that constitute water: He changed water into wine. (See John 2.) And he commanded the elements acting up on the Sea of Galilee: "He arose, and rebuked the wind and the raging of the water: and they ceased, and there was a calm. . . . And they being afraid wondered, saying one to another, What manner of man is this! for he commandeth even the winds and water, and they obey him." (Luke 8:24–25.) Should it be surprising that the same God who organized the elements in the beginning, who exhibited his divine power by parting the waters of the Red Sea, and who later caused miraculous control of the flow of the Jordan could control the water of a small lake in Galilee?

The physical commodity called water was definitely involved in the words and works of Jesus, but the more significant use of water was its symbolic use. The saying "From water comes all life" also refers to creation. In the beginning of this world's creation, the earth was covered with water. (See Gen. 1:1–9.) All physical creations emerged after that water cover. It was covered a second time during the days of Noah, and all creatures once again emerged from a water cover. (See Gen. 7–8.) Human beings are born from a water cover in the womb. And it is water that sustains all life forms.

With the Flood, the earth received its baptism, the water being used as a cleansing agent to restore the earth from its degraded condition. Jesus taught that humankind must also be immersed in water to be restored or saved from their degenerate conditions. "I say unto thee, Except a man be born of water and of the Spirit, he cannot enter into the kingdom of God." (John 3:5.)

Peter pursued the comparison of the Flood with individual immersion for removal of sin: " . . . in the days of Noah, while the ark was a preparing, wherein few, that is, eight souls were saved by water. The like figure whereunto even baptism doth also now save us (not the putting away of the filth of the flesh, but the answer of a good conscience toward God)." (1 Pet. 3:20–21.) The physical properties of water are not meant to cleanse the soul, but the symbolic act of submission, of lowering oneself into the water, shows contrition and a desire to be cleansed from sin. The immersion, accompanied by genuine repentance, accomplishes the cleansing.

*"All the Jews, except they wash their hands oft, eat not." (Mark 7:3.)*

In addition to baptism, there are two other instances where water was used as a cleansing agent: on one's hands and on one's feet. For physical hygiene, hands were to be washed before eating a meal. "When they saw some of his disciples eat bread with defiled, that is to say, with unwashen, hands, they found fault. For the Pharisees, and all the Jews, except they wash their hands oft, eat not, holding the tradition of the elders." (Mark 7:2–3.)

Besides the usual physical cleansing, the laws of purification demanded that a *ritual* cleansing be performed frequently, but some Jews by Jesus' day had carried the ceremony of cleansing so far that its symbolic, spiritual purpose had lost much of its efficacy. Jesus thus remonstrated against not the law itself but the traditions that arose around the law. The custom of ritual washing was so common in those days that it does not surprise us to see even a gentile imitating such a symbolic act: "When Pilate saw that he could prevail nothing, but that rather a tumult was made, he took water, and washed his hands before the multitude." (Matt. 27:24.)

The hands, along with the heart, were used more than any other part of the body in imagery. Hands represent power, control, or agency. He that would ascend into the hill of the Lord, or stand in the holy temple, is "he that hath clean hands and a pure heart." (Ps. 24:3–4.) James wrote, "Draw nigh to God, and he will draw nigh to you. Cleanse your hands . . . and purify your hearts." (James 4:8.)

### "Ye also ought to wash one another's feet." (John 13:14.)

Another part of the body that was washed with water was the feet. Feet were symbolic of the path one took in life. They could represent evil ways: "[This thing] doth the Lord hate: . . . feet that be swift in running to mischief." (Prov. 6:16, 18.) They also represent the way one should walk: "Thy word is a lamp unto my feet, and a light unto my path." (Ps. 119:105.)

As a courtesy to guests, a servant was usually stationed at the doorway to wash the dusty feet of those invited to special feasts and other occasions. "[Jesus] said unto Simon, Seest thou this woman? I entered into thine house, thou gavest me no water for my feet: but she hath washed my feet with tears, and wiped them with the hairs of her head." (Luke 7:44.)

Jesus gave higher meaning to the washing of feet when "he poureth water into a bason, and began to wash the disciples' feet." (John 13:5.) He later explained, "Know ye what I have done to you? Ye call me Master and Lord: and ye say well; for so I am. If I then, your Lord and Master, have washed your feet; ye also ought to wash one another's feet. For I have given you an example, that ye should do as I have done to you. . . . The servant is not greater than his lord; neither he that is sent greater than he that sent

him." (John 13:12–16.) The washing with water was symbolic of the service that the leaders were to render to those under their stewardship; the greatest were really the servants of all.

### "Doth a fountain send forth at the same place sweet water and bitter?" (James 3:11.)

The most effective and favorite form of teaching in the ancient Near East was to illustrate something in human conduct with something in nature. Comparison was the heart of Semitic literary expression. Jesus compared the life-style he espoused to spiritual drink. Since water is so vital to the bodily systems, it is an appropriate analogy to speak of drinking deeply from spiritual waters that satiate the inner and eternal thirsts of man. "Whosoever drinketh of the water that I shall give him shall never thirst; but the water that I shall give him shall be in him a well of water springing up into everlasting life." (John 4:14.) "He that believeth on me, . . . out of his belly shall flow rivers of living water." (John 7:38.)

Cisterns and pools are artificially developed containers or reservoirs for storage of water from another source. They are subject to stagnation and pollution. Wells, springs, and rivers, on the other hand, may be "living," that is, *flowing*—a continual supply of refreshing and life-giving water. For instance, Amos had pleaded, "Let judgment run down as waters, and righteousness as a mighty [Hebrew, *never-failing*] stream." (Amos 5:24.)

Centuries before Jesus, Jeremiah saw

*Top:* The Pool of Bethesda, where Jesus healed a paralyzed man (see John 5), as shown in the model city of New Testament Jerusalem at the Holyland Hotel, Jerusalem. *Center left:* Ancient well with centuries-old rope marks visible. *Center right:* Saltwater channel along the west shore of the Sea of Galilee. *Bottom left:* A scene from the life of Jesus being filmed (Genesis Project, 1978) near Magdala on the west shore of the Sea of Galilee. *Bottom right:* Remains of an aqueduct that transported water to ancient Caesarea from four miles away.

the Lord lamenting the condition of his people: "They have forsaken me the fountain of living waters, and hewed them out cisterns, broken cisterns, that can hold no water." (Jer. 2:13.) The Israelites in the Assyrian and Babylonian periods had rejected their Source of ongoing revelation and guidance. The perpetual replenishment of their spiritual waters, which God was willing to provide, had been superseded by his people's desire to horde the waters of life they had already received and to store them away in underground cisterns of tradition and ceremonialism. The waters stored away, though no longer a perennial supply, could still have sustained and satisfied them for a time had they been put into undamaged cisterns, but alas, the cisterns themselves were marred and broken and could hold no water.

Peter taught that those who abandon the Source of life are "wells without water" (2 Pet. 2:17), and Jude rejoined, "Clouds they are without water, carried about of winds" (1:12).

On avoiding hypocrisy and living with integrity, James metaphorically inquired, "Doth a fountain send forth at the same place sweet water and bitter? Can the fig tree . . . bear olive berries? either a vine, figs? so can no fountain both yield salt water and fresh." (James 3:11–12.) The image is fittingly drawn from the background and experiences of these disciples. At various points up and down the Jordan Valley, a seismic region, particularly around the Sea of Galilee, there are mineral springs and freshwater springs. Even today the salty springwater is channeled

south away from the lake, which is modern Israel's central drinking-water reservoir. Sweet water and bitter water are not a felicitous mix, nor is a conscientious life compatible with a devious one.

*"Jesus went over the sea of Galilee, which is the sea of Tiberias." (John 6:1.)*

There are four seas inside or bordering the land of Jesus. Three of them are mentioned in the New Testament. Though well known, the Dead Sea, or the Salt Sea as it was called, is not specifically referred to, nor does it figure in any story. The Red Sea is mentioned in connection with the miracle the Lord performed for the ancient Israelites departing from Egypt. (See Acts 7:36.) The Mediterranean is described simply as "the sea" in the accounts of Jesus visiting Tyre and Sidon (see Luke 6:17) and Peter visiting Simon the tanner in Joppa (see Acts 10:6, 32).

The Sea of Galilee is alluded to more than forty times, either by the name "Galilee," "Tiberias," or "Gennesaret." Luke sometimes called it a "lake" (Greek, *limne*) rather than a "sea" (Greek, *thalassa*). Technically the small body of water, which is less than eight miles wide and about twelve miles long, is a lake, but the Hebrew term *yam* may be translated as either "lake" or "sea." The Sea of Galilee lies in the Rift Valley nearly seven hundred feet below sea level, making it the lowest freshwater lake in the world. Around its shores, especially to the north and west, most of Jesus' ministry occurred.

The rivers included in the narratives of Jesus' life are the Jordan, which runs into and out of the Sea of Galilee, and the Kidron, which is only a seasonal stream where it begins at Jerusalem. No springs are specifically cited.

*"There shall meet you a man bearing a pitcher of water." (Mark 14:13.)*

Instruments used for drawing, carrying, and storing water were earthenware pitchers and pots. Instructing two disciples about how to find the room ready for his Passover meal, Jesus said, "Go ye into the city, and there shall meet you a man bearing a pitcher of water: follow him." (Mark 14:13.) After Jesus' conversation with a Samaritan woman at Jacob's Well, "the woman then left her waterpot, and went her way into the city." (John 4:28.)

At the wedding feast where Jesus would perform his first recorded public miracle, "there were set there six waterpots of stone, . . . containing two or three firkins apiece." (John 2:6.) Waterpots in this case were also used for wine. A firkin was approximately nine gallons, so the six pots could have contained between a hundred and a hundred and fifty gallons, supplying a large wedding celebration. Though pots were often made of clay, there were also pots of stone. The porous nature of a pot made from clay or limestone allowed for evaporation, which cooled the liquid contents. Several stone pots from the Roman period are on permanent display in the Israel Museum in Jerusalem.

# CLIMATE, WEATHER, AND NATURAL PHENOMENA

*"Summer is now nigh at hand."*
*(Luke 21:30.)*

The land of Jesus has only two seasons: the hot, dry season (summer) and the cold, wet season (winter). There are transitional periods between them when the weather fluctuates quite unpredictably, but generally it is either one or the other. The New Testament reflects this weather regime, mentioning these two seasons only. During late winter (usually in March) the fig tree issues its first tiny leaves, signaling the beginning of the warm season. "Now learn a parable of the fig tree; When his branch is yet tender, and putteth forth leaves, ye know that summer is nigh." (Matt. 24:32; see also Luke 21:29–30.)

Most of the pilgrimage festivals of the Jews were scheduled during the transitional periods between the two seasons, when it was neither too wet and cold nor too dry and hot for travel. One of the feasts, however, fell during the wintertime. Jesus was teaching in the Temple, "and it was at Jerusalem the feast of the dedication, and it was winter." (John 10:22.) The Feast of the Dedication (Hebrew, *Hanukkah)* celebrates the rededica-

tion of the Temple under Judah the Maccabee. The feast began on the twenty-fifth of Chisleu, roughly our month of December, during which time the weather can still be mild, just before the heavy winter rains begin (normally in January.)

When teaching about some of the signs of the last days and the associated destruction and desolation that would come upon Jerusalem, Jesus warned his disciples, "Pray ye that your flight be not in the winter." (Matt. 24:20; Mark 13:18.) Being cast out into the blustery elements in wintertime, subject to the cold blasts of wind and rain whipping over the tops of the Judaean hills, could be miserable and tragic indeed.

Passover is celebrated each year at the end of the winter, at the time of resurrection of all the floral world, the season of renewal we call spring. Passover days can be lovely and warm, but the nights can still be chilling. Jesus' last mortal week in Jerusalem was during the Passover. It was cool at night in the Garden of Gethsemane; Caiaphas' palace was cold. "The servants and officers stood there, who had made a fire of coals; for it was cold: and they warmed themselves: and Peter stood with them, and warmed himself." (John 18:18.)

### "When the sun was up, they were scorched." (Matt. 13:6.)

In the Mediterranean subtropical climate of the land of Israel, the sun can beat down with merciless constancy. Summer days follow one after another, on and on with unrelenting cloudlessness. The sun's rays fall hard on the earth, scorching any seed or plant that has no root, causing it to wither away. (See Matt. 13:6.) James saw a parallel in the transitoriness of riches: "For the sun is no sooner risen with a burning heat, but it withereth the grass, and the flower thereof falleth, and the grace of the fashion of it perisheth: so also shall the rich man fade away in his ways." (James 1:11.)

Outside labor was physically taxing under the summer sun. In one of Jesus' parables, those who were hired early in the morning complained about equal payment being given to those who had hired on late in the day. "These last have wrought but one hour, and thou hast made them equal unto us, which have borne the burden and heat of the day." (Matt. 20:12.)

### "Ye can discern the face of the sky." (Matt. 16:3.)

The ancients knew how to read the sky for probable weather conditions. After the long half year of changeless summer sky, the rain clouds begin to appear. Colors burst across earth's canopy in the morning or hang onto wide portions of the evening sky, portending their various changes in the weather.

Jesus contrasted that ability to anticipate the weather with the inability to see God's signs: "When it is evening, ye say, It will be fair weather: for the sky is red. And in the morning, It will be foul weather to day: for the sky is red and lowring [threatening]. O ye hypocrites, ye can discern the face of the sky; but can ye not discern the signs of the times?" (Matt. 16:2–3.)

### "When ye see a cloud rise out of the west, straightway ye say, There cometh a shower; and so it is." (Luke 12:54.)

The Mediterranean Sea is the focal point of the Levantine storm systems. Evaporation off the great sea has been measured in our modern day to average one hundred thousand tons of water per second! Winter winds pick up moisture from the sea and carry rain-laden clouds eastward over the land. When the clouds meet the mountains and hills running north-south through the coastal countries, they are forced to ascend. As they rise, they part with some of their water load in the form of rain. Once past the mountains, air currents descend, and with a warmer terrain in the Judaean Desert and Rift Valley, little precipitation occurs, until the clouds move eastward to the hills of Transjordan and part with most of the remaining moisture.

Thus, once over the land, clouds dump their water load generously on the coastal lands and western slopes of the hill country, whereas the eastern slopes are left in what is known as a "rain shadow," or topographical desert. The general pattern is rain and fertility in the northern and western regions, and dry desert lands to the east and south. Jerusalem averages twenty-two to twenty-five inches of rain per year, as much as or more than London, Athens, Vienna, or Paris. The peculiarity is the duration—Jerusalem receiving most of its annual rainfall in the two-month period from mid-January to mid-March.

Rain was an obsessive concern of the ancient inhabitants of the Levant. Egypt had the Nile, and Mesopotamia, the Tigris and Euphrates. Peoples of the eastern Mediterranean coastlands, however, had no assured water source. Actually, they *did* have a constant water source: the Lord made it clear that his heavens were open to pour out all the moisture they needed, based on their obedience.

If they kept his commandments they received the rain in its due season. (See Deut. 11:13–14.) That promise of rain was important enough to be one of four passages sealed up in frontlets (phylacteries) between their eyes and placed on the doorposts (mezuzas) of their houses. (See Deut. 11:18–20.) The land in which they lived was a testing ground of their obedience, and with his people's faithfulness, the Lord God was pleased to respond. "He did good, and gave us rain from heaven, and fruitful seasons, filling our hearts with food and gladness." (Acts 14:17.)

Israelites grew up watching the annual cycle of storms: the first (or "former") rains in October-November, the rainy season from January-March, and the "latter" rains in April-May. (See Deut. 11:14; Jer. 5:24; Joel 2:23.) First rains served to loosen the soil after the long, hot summer and prepare it for planting, and the latter rain, some weeks after the heavy winter rains had passed, kept the crops growing until the harvest time approached. "Be patient therefore, brethren, unto the coming of the Lord. Behold, the husbandman waiteth for the precious fruit of the earth, and hath long patience for it, until he receive the early and latter rain." (James 5:7.)

Israelite history included the well-known story of Elijah cursing the land with three and a half years of famine (famine meaning "no rain"). After challenging the priests of Baal on top of Mount Carmel, Elijah sent his servant seven times to look west toward the sea, and finally he spotted "a little cloud out of the sea, like a man's hand . . . [and soon] the heaven was black with clouds and wind, and there was a great rain." (1 Kgs. 18:44–45.) James recounted Elijah's miraculous control of elements: "He prayed earnestly that it might not rain: and it rained not on the earth by the space of three years and six months. And he prayed again, and the heaven gave rain, and the earth brought forth her fruit." (James 5:17–18.)

Jesus also made use of the meteorological pattern to illustrate his teaching. "When ye see a cloud rise out of the west, straightway ye say, There cometh a shower; and so it is." (Luke 12:54.) Concluding his sermon on the mount, Jesus taught a parable contrasting the merits of building a house on rock or on sand. The house being built, of course, was a human life. Our lives, he taught, should not be built on the shifty, listless sands but on a rock, or *the* rock (the Greek text has a def-

59

inite article), meaning we should build our lives upon the Lord, the Rock of our Salvation.

"The rain descended, and the floods came, and the winds blew, and beat upon that house; and it fell not." (Matt. 7:25.) Rains come from above, floods from below, and winds from the sides—and when temptations and trials come at us from above, from beneath, and from all sides, our lives will not fall apart if we have built firmly on the Rock.

### "The sea arose by reason of a great wind that blew." (John 6:18.)

The Sea of Galilee lies deep in the Rift Valley, nearly seven hundred feet below the level of the Mediterranean. It is surrounded by hills that are above sea level on all sides except the south. As winds sweep down the western slopes, they can stir up waves on the small lake with considerable ferocity. Seasoned fishermen can still be struck with fear and panic if caught in a tempest in the middle of the lake.

Gospel writers recorded several instances when violent storms came up on the Sea of Galilee: "There arose a great tempest in the sea, insomuch that the ship was covered with the waves." (Matt. 8:24.) "There arose a great storm of wind, and the waves beat into the ship." (Mark 4:37.) "There came down a storm of wind on the lake; and they were filled with water, and were in jeopardy." (Luke 8:23.) "The sea arose by reason of a great wind that blew." (John 6:18; see Matt. 14:24; Mark 6:47–48.)

James metaphorically illustrates the power of the small but impulsive tongue by comparing it with the strong winds that rise on the Mediterranean, "Behold also the ships, which though they be so great, and are driven of fierce winds, yet are they turned about with a very small helm, whithersoever the governor listeth." (James 3:4.)

### "When ye see the south wind blow, ye say, There will be heat; and it cometh to pass." (Luke 12:55.)

Jonah sat under his gourd vine east of the city of Nineveh for only a short time. Some kind of pest attacked the gourd, and it withered. When the sun came up, "God prepared a vehement east wind; and the sun beat upon the head of Jonah, that he fainted, and wished in himself to die, and said, It is better for me to die than to live." (Jonah 4:8.) What kind of wind could be so enervating as to make a man want to die?

The Eastern Mediterranean states are encompassed on the east and on the south by great deserts. Barometric lows or depressions over Libya and Egypt can draw strong, dry winds off the eastern and southern deserts and over the land of Israel. The condition is known in Arabic as *khamsin* (which means fifty, from the tradition that a year has fifty days with *khamsin* conditions). A scientific name for the wind is sirocco (or scirocco), an Italian word that derives from the Arabic *sharkiyeh*, meaning east wind. Whether from the east or the south, it is the same phenomenon—a wind that comes off the deserts carrying fine dust that impairs visibility, raises temperatures, and dissipates human energy.

*Top left:* A tiny plant survives in the sun-baked earth only if it sinks firm roots for nourishment. *Top right:* Winter storm clouds — the "first rain" (Deut. 11:14) — are the temporal salvation of a thirsty land. *Center left:* Strong winds can stir up waves and fishermen's fears on the small lake of Galilee. *Center right:* Mount Hermon, the highest mountain in the Holy Land, is covered with snow much of the year. *Bottom left:* Crack in an immersion pool at Qumran, caused by an earthquake in 31 B.C.

The word "heat" in the previous sub-head is translated in the Revised Standard Version as "scorching heat." The Hebrew word *sharav* is the root word meaning parch or scorch (by the sun). This weather condition occurs mostly during the unpredictable transitional periods of April to May and September to October and affects water sources, agriculture (and therefore the economy), and personal behavior.

Once again Jesus used some phenomena in nature to emphasize his teaching: his people could tell that, when clouds formed in the west, it was going to rain and that, when the south wind began to blow, there would be a khamsin. "Ye can discern the face of the sky and of the earth; but how is it that ye do not discern this time?" (Luke 12:54–56.)

*"His countenance was like lightning, and his raiment white as snow."*
*(Matt. 28:3.)*

Lightning is the sudden and awe-inspiring force of nature that the ancients saw as a manifestation of God's power in the heavens. Along with the earthquake, the fierce storm with its loud claps of thunder and jagged flashes of lightning could strike terror and a sense of helplessness in the heart of man. Lightning was one of the phenomena of nature dramatic enough to remind man of his puniness and dependence on heaven.

Throughout the Bible, lightning is associated with the *Shekhinah*, the presence of God, as in the theophany on Mount Sinai, or with the appearance of a messenger from God, as in the above subhead scripture describing an angel who ap-

peared at Jesus' tomb and frightened the Roman guards so much that they "became as dead men." (Matt. 28:4.) When a messenger from heaven appeared on earth, the prophet or historian would try to describe the sight with such words as *brilliant, exquisite, brighter than the noonday sun,* and so on. Paul, in telling of the vision of the Lord that converted him, used these phrases: "from heaven a great light" (Acts 22:6) and "a light from heaven, above the brightness of the sun" (Acts 26:13).

Luke described the physical change that came over Jesus on the Mount of Transfiguration: "As he prayed, the fashion of his countenance was altered, and his raiment was white and glistering." (Luke 9:29.) The Greek term translated here as "glistering" means "as lightning." Matthew says he was "transfigured before them: and his face did shine as the sun, and his raiment was white." (Matt. 17:2.) The energy that radiates from a heavenly being is so splendid and refulgent that mortals must use the most elevated vocabulary at their command to describe it.

"For as the lightning, that lighteneth out of the one part under heaven, shineth unto the other part under heaven; so shall also the Son of man be in his day." (Luke 17:24.) According to the King James Version, Matthew, as Luke did, used *lightning* to describe the second coming of the Savior: "For as the lightning cometh out of the east, and shineth even unto the west; so shall also the coming of the Son of man be." (24:27.)

That analogy from nature—Jesus coming as lightning from the east—is a brilliant and powerful image but meteorologically incorrect. In the Holy Land, lightning does not come from the east. Lightning, as with all storm clouds and precipitation, originates in the *west*, from over the Mediterranean. The Prophet Joseph Smith (who, of course, had no training in Near Eastern weather patterns) corrected the prophecy to read: "For as the *light of the morning* cometh out of the east, and shineth even unto the west, and covereth the whole earth; so shall also the coming of the Son of Man be." (JST, Matt. 24:27; italics added.)

Another term used in describing extraterrestrial beings is *snow*. The whiteness of snow covering the earth, especially under the full power of the midday sun, is so brilliant as to seem painful to look upon. It was the ultimate in earthly lustre. In describing the God of heaven, the apostle John envisioned and wrote that "his head and his hairs were . . . as white as snow." (Rev. 1:14.) Mark also adopts a brilliant image in his word picture of the transfiguration of Jesus: "His raiment became shining, exceeding white as snow; so as no fuller on earth can white them." (Mark 9:3.)

Jesus' clothing was whiter, then, than newly made wool or linen. The fuller, who usually had his workshop near a spring, the water source in a city, worked with his soap to clean cloth, ridding it of all stains to make it white. But no fuller could approach the gleaming brightness of sunluminated snow, and no snow could approach the splendor of a transfigured being.

Though much of the Holy Land is arid desert, yet the high central hills do experience snowfall. Jerusalem averages two days of snow each year. It usually falls lightly and melts away quickly, but during this century Jerusalem has seen heavy snow: in February 1950, over two feet, and in February 1920, over three feet. The highest mountain, Mount Hermon, at over 9,200 feet, has a snow cover much of the year.

## " . . . when great famine was throughout all the land." (Luke 4:25.)

Gospel writers mention famine a number of times. In his speech before the Sanhedrin, Stephen recalled the famine in the days of Abraham, "Now there came a dearth over all the land of Egypt and Chanaan, and great affliction: and our fathers found no sustenance." (Acts 7:11.) And Jesus, speaking to the local congregation in the synagogue at Nazareth, recalled the famine in the days of Elijah, "when the heaven was shut up three years and six months, when great famine was throughout all the land." (Luke 4:25.)

The condition "heaven was shut up" is the precursor to most famine conditions. Other causes, such as prolonged military sieges, disease, or pestilence brought on by insects, especially locusts, could result in famine, but the usual cause in Bible lands was drought—heaven (not the sky, but *heaven*) was shut. The prophets made it clear that heaven would open again through humble faithfulness.

In the parable of the prodigal son, Jesus raised a hypothetical situation of the profligate son who wasted his inheritance and found himself in the direst of conditions, "When he had spent all, there arose a mighty famine in that land; and he began to be in want." (Luke 15:14.) But famine was not just a hypothetical situation for inhabitants of the lands of the Bible—it was a very real possibility. With little or no rain, vast portions of the land could experience crop failure, with subsequent pressures on the economy. The common people would be unable to sustain minimal life needs. The famine arising in the parable, then, recalled in the minds of its hearers a very real, immediate danger, illustrating how truly foolish wasting one's living can be.

We have no specific reference to famine during Jesus' lifetime, but a few years after his departure: "There stood up one of [the disciples] named Agabus, and signified by the spirit that there should be great dearth throughout all the world [that is, throughout their localized Mediterranean world]: which came to pass in the days of Claudius Caesar." (Acts 11:28.) We have additional historical attestation of this very famine, which did occur in the Roman Empire during the reign of Claudius (A.D. 41–54). The famine hit Judaea in A.D. 46.[1] "Then the disciples, every man according to his ability, determined to send relief unto the brethren which dwelt in Judaea." (Acts 11:29.)

### "The earth did quake, and the rocks rent." (Matt. 27:51.)

Some natural disasters may have been partly avoidable, but the ancients knew no way of predicting or controlling an earthquake. Since the most dramatic feature of the land of Jesus was the Rift Valley

running north-south its full length, seismic disturbances were common enough that the people of the Near East had either experienced or heard about one or more in their lifetimes (particularly one in 31 B.C. that killed over thirty thousand people in Judaea alone).

Surprisingly, only one earthquake is explicitly mentioned in the Old Testament. The ministry of the prophet Amos was dated in the superscription to his writings as "two years before the earthquake." (Amos 1:1.) That earthquake in the days of Uzziah was apparently so severe that it was used for some time to date historical events. It was of such unusual intensity and inflicted such devastation that the memory of it survived for over two and a half centuries. In Zechariah 14:5, it served as a pattern of extremely destructive earthquakes: "Ye shall flee, like as ye fled from the earthquake in the days of Uzziah king of Judah." We may infer that that particular earthquake wreaked destruction in the Jerusalem region and in Bethel, and archaeological excavations have found pointed evidence of it in the ruins of Beersheba in the south, Hazor in the north, and Deir Alla in the eastern Jordan Valley.

Clear reference is made to an earthquake at the time of Jesus' death: "Jesus, when he had cried again with a loud voice, yielded up the ghost. And, behold, the veil of the temple was rent in twain from the top to the bottom; and the earth did quake, and the rocks rent; and the graves were opened. . . . Now when the centurion, and they that were with him, watching Jesus, saw the earthquake, and those things that were done, they feared greatly, saying, Truly this was the Son of God." (Matt. 27:50–54.)

On the third day an aftershock was recorded: "In the end of the sabbath, as it began to dawn toward the first day of the week, came Mary Magdalene and the other Mary to see the sepulchre. And, be-

hold, there was a great earthquake." (Matt. 28:1–2.)

### NOTE

1. See Josephus, *Antiquities,* XX.51; Tacitus, *Annals,* XII.43; Suetonius, *Claudius,* 18.

# MINERALS AND ORES

*"The stone which the builders rejected, the same is become the head of the corner." (Matt. 21:42.)*

Inhabitants of the land of Jesus were, of course, familiar with the rock under their feet. The sedimentary limestone in the central hills of Judaea and Samaria and the hard black basalt spewed over the Galilee region by volcanoes on the Golan Heights were used as building stone and for a variety of other purposes. Royal palaces and public buildings, city walls, synagogues, and the temple itself were made of stone. "As he went out of the temple, one of his disciples saith unto him, Master, see what manner of stones and what buildings are here!" (Mark 13:1.)

Mention of stone is found throughout the New Testament. Jesus performed his first recorded miracle with the "six waterpots of stone" (John 2:6); at Jesus' death, Joseph of Arimathea laid the Lord's body in a "sepulchre that was hewn in stone" (Luke 23:53) and "rolled a great stone to the door of the sepulchre" (Matt. 27:60); and Paul spoke of the great commandments given at Sinai on "tables of stone" (2 Cor. 3:3). House builders would dig deep and lay the foundations on rock. (See

Luke 6:48.) Rocky soil was what farmers had to plant their seeds in, and the ones that fell on rock developed no roots and soon lacked moisture and withered away. (See Luke 8:6, 13.)

From experiences in Jesus' life and from his teachings, we learn of the availability of stone and its uses (fortunate or unfortunate): "When the tempter came to him, he said, If thou be the Son of God, command that these stones be made bread." (Matt. 4:3.) "He shall give his angels charge concerning thee . . . lest at any time thou dash thy foot against a stone." (Matt. 4:6.) "What man is there of you, whom if his son ask bread, will he give him a stone?" (Matt. 7:9.) "Always, night and day, he was in the mountains, and in the tombs, crying, and cutting himself with stones." (Mark 5:5.) "I tell you that, if these should hold their peace, the stones would immediately cry out." (Luke 19:40.)

Because the Mosaic laws countenanced it, and because they were plentiful, rocks were still used in the Roman period to kill people. From a parable of Jesus: "He sent unto them another servant; and at him they cast stones, and wounded him in the head." (Mark 12:4.) Actual instances include the following: "All the people will stone us: for they be persuaded that John was a prophet." (Luke 20:6.) "He lifted up himself, and said unto them, He that is without sin among you, let him first cast a stone at her." (John 8:7.) "Then took they up stones to cast at him [Jesus]." (John 8:59; see 10:31.) "They stoned Stephen." (Acts 7:59.)

Thus we find a variety of uses of stone at the time, some beneficent, some malevolent. But there was a higher use of rock or stone. The prophets and Jesus used it as a teaching tool, an image or symbol. David in former times had uttered the following: "The Lord is my rock . . . ; in him will I trust. . . . Who is a rock save our God? God is my strength and power." (2 Sam. 22:2–3, 32–33.) The Psalmist had sung: "In the time of trouble he shall hide me in his pavilion: . . . he shall set me up upon a rock." (Ps. 27:5.) "Be thou my strong rock, for an house of defence to save me. For thou art my rock and my fortress." (Ps. 31:2–3.) "He only is my rock and my salvation: he is my defence; I shall not be moved." (Ps. 62:6.)

From these Old Testament passages, we know that rock and stone were used to denote something solid, firm, and immovable. That definition carries over into the New Testament. "Jesus saith unto them, Did ye never read in the scriptures [Ps. 118:22], The stone which the builders rejected, the same is become the head of the corner?" (Matt. 21:42.) "It is contained in the scripture [Isa. 28:16], Behold, I lay in Sion a chief corner stone, elect, pre-

cious." (1 Pet. 2:6.) The household of God was "built upon the foundation of the apostles and prophets, Jesus Christ himself being the chief corner stone." (Eph. 2:20.)

The cornerstone (Hebrew, *rosh pinna* = literally, head of the corner) was a large stone placed in a corner of the building's foundation to secure it, to provide stability and strength for the structure (at least symbolically), and to serve as a guide for all other foundation stones. New Testament writers saw in Jesus (as the Messiah) the fulfillment of this prophetic analogy: "This is the stone which was set at nought of you builders, which is become the head of the corner." (Acts 4:11.)

The Messiah is he who gives firmness and sturdiness to the household of God, but something as solid and immovable as a rock can also be a stumblingblock: "The stone which the builders disallowed, the same is made the head of the corner, and a stone of stumbling, and a rock of offence, even to them which stumble at the word, being disobedient." (1 Pet. 2:7–8; see Rom. 9:33.) "Whosoever shall fall on this stone shall be broken [become humbled, contrite]: but on whomsoever it shall fall, it will grind him to powder." (Matt. 21:44.)

Following Jesus' ascension into heaven, Peter became the head of the household of God on earth. When Peter had first been introduced to the Lord, Jesus announced a symbolic change in his name: "When Jesus beheld him, he said, Thou art Simon the son of Jona: thou shalt be called Cephas, which is by interpretation, a stone." (John 1:42.) The name Peter comes from Greek *petros*, which means literally rock. The Aramaic equivalent is Cephas (*Kepha*), which also means rock.

Here we have identified the three main languages used in the land at the time of Jesus. His chief apostle was to be known neither by his Hebrew name Shimon or Simeon, nor by his Greek name Petros, but by his Aramaic apellation Cephas. The renaming foreshadowed the apostle's future role. In guiding the early Church as its chief prophet, seer, and revelator, Peter (Cephas) would provide strength and stability to the fledgling organization. The Prophet Joseph Smith inserted into John 1:42 the following significant change: "Thou shalt be called Cephas, which is, by interpretation, *a seer, or a stone*." (Italics added.) We recall that Jesus gave the keys of the kingdom, the commission of leadership, to Peter the Rock at Caesarea Philippi, at the foot of the most massive rock formation in the country.

## "As the sand which is by the sea shore innumerable . . . " (Heb. 11:12.)

Biblical writers tapped all elements of nature for their metaphors. Not only did they compare water, climatic conditions, and the stone of the hills with the human experience, but they also used the sands of the deserts and the Mediterranean coast to illustrate their messages. Sand, which is simply an accumulation of fine particles of rock, is adapted in the New Testament primarily to two different senses: the quantity of Israelites and the contrast to rock for a building foundation.

In Genesis 32:12, for example, the Lord had promised Jacob, "I will surely do thee good, and make thy seed as the sand of the sea, which cannot be numbered for multitude." Paul perpetuated the image, "The number of the children of Israel be as the sand of the sea." (Rom. 9:27.) The most famous reference to sand is Jesus' contrast to building on solid rock, where the foolish man built his house on shifty, listless, and unstable sand. (See Matt. 7:26.)

## "A man that is called Jesus made clay, and anointed mine eyes." (John 9:11.)

Clay is a malleable composition of earth combined with moisture. It was used for centuries in making pottery, writing tablets, bricks, household objects, toys, and statuettes for worshiping local deities. Vessels were made of many different materials like ivory, wood, brass, iron, marble (see Rev. 18:12), and gold and silver (see 2 Tim. 2:20), but no material was so accessible as earth itself, so most vessels were earthen vessels (see 2 Cor. 4:7; 2 Tim. 2:20). These pottery vessels were useful in holding water, wine, olive oil (see Matt. 25:4), vinegar (see John 19:29), fish (see Matt. 13:48), and many other commodities. Clay could also be fired into roof tiles: "When they could not find by what way they might bring him in because of the multitude, they went upon the housetop, and let him down through the tiling [Greek, *keramos* = English, *ceramic*] with his couch into the midst before Jesus." (Luke 5:19.)

Jesus used a simple kind of clay or mud to anoint the eyes of a blind man, thereby involving him physically in the miracle: "When he had thus spoken, he spat on

69

*Top left:* Hexagonal basalt formation at the Sea of Galilee near the Plain of Bethsaida. *Top right:* Limestone in the hill country of Judaea. *Center left:* The posterity of the Patriarchs and the number of the Israelites were prophesied to be as numerous as the sand in the deserts or by the seashore. *Center right:* A potter shaping clay vessels in modern-day Hebron. *Bottom left:* Salt, the great preservative, was mined from the southern end of the Dead Sea or extracted from the water itself.

the ground, and made clay of the spittle, and he anointed the eyes of the blind man with the clay." The man later testified, "He put clay upon mine eyes, and I washed, and do see." (John 9:6, 15.)

The most impressive symbolic use of clay in the Old Testament was Jeremiah's comparison of the Lord to the master Potter, trying to mold his people Israel into their most beautiful and useful shape: "O house of Israel, cannot I do with you as this potter? saith the Lord. Behold, as the clay is in the potter's hand, so are ye in mine hand." (Jer. 18:6; see 18:1–6.) The Lord God, who made the body-clay of every human soul, wants his children to be as pliable as clay and to allow his divine hand to work each one into a vessel of righteousness. Those who persist intractable or recalcitrant, "as the vessels of a potter shall they be broken in shivers." (Rev. 2:27.)

*"An alabaster box of ointment . . . "*
*(Luke 7:37.)*

While Jesus was eating at the house of Simon the leper in Bethany, a woman came with an alabaster box containing costly perfume, and "she brake the box, and poured it on his head." (Mark 14:3.) Alabaster was a translucent stone, well known to the ancient Egyptians (Tutankhamen's tomb, for instance, contained many beautifully carved alabaster boxes) and circulated throughout the Near East, though at some expense. The particular vessel in question was used as a perfume flask. The long, narrow neck or the seal placed on it had to be broken before the perfume could be poured out.

*"A lake of fire burning with*
*brimstone . . . " (Rev. 19:20.)*

In English, we speak of "far and near," "law and order," and "trials and tribulations." Such standard combinations of words or word pairs are also evident in Ugaritic, Hebrew, and other ancient Near Eastern languages, like silver and gold, day and night, and ox and ass. Similarly, we often find in scripture the word pair *fire and brimstone.*

Of the eight instances of fire and brimstone in the New Testament, seven are in the book of Revelation, where its use portends torment and punishment in the last days for the wicked. Brimstone is sulphur, a yellow-green, highly combustible element commonly found along the shores of the Dead Sea. The same substance is used to make matches and gunpowder and other products today in the chemical and paper industries. When ignited with fire, sulphur liquifies and produces a sharp and suffocating burning odor that can desolate and kill. Apparently in those days, no harsher picture of the hellish fate of the wicked could be portrayed than that of being thrown into a lake of fire burning with brimstone: "The fearful, and unbelieving, and the abominable, and murderers, and whoremongers, and sorcerers, and idolaters, and all liars, shall have their part in the lake which burneth with fire and brimstone." (Rev. 21:8.)

*"Ye are the salt of the earth." (Matt.*
*5:13.)*

In an age without refrigerators, salt was the great preservative. In a memorable metaphor, Jesus calls his disciples salt: they would preserve his teachings and life-style among the peoples of the earth, but if they lost their conscientiousness in following his example, they would be worthless in his kingdom and would be cast out, as useless salt is cast out. (See Matt. 5:13.)

Salt is plentiful. It is calculated that the evaporation of one cubic mile of seawater would leave about 140 million tons of salts, most of which would be sodium chloride or common salt. Salt was mined in Bible times from the hills and earth at the southern end of the Dead Sea, particularly from Mount Sedom, which is a salt mountain. Otherwise, it could be extracted from the Salt Sea waters themselves, but with care to remove impurities and poisonous elements contained in those waters, which are heavy with various minerals.

Salt does not lose its savor with age. It is lost through mixture and contamination. The Lord's metaphor in the above subhead may be a warning to avoid any alteration of God-given teachings or admixture with the philosophies of men or the corrupting influences of those who love evil. The encouragement is for disciples to maintain a pure and undefiled gospel and to season the world with their tasteful living. "Salt is good: but if the salt have lost his saltness, wherewith will ye season it [bring back its saltiness]? Have salt in yourselves, and have peace one with another." (Mark 9:50.)

In the handbook for Levitical priests, the Lord had commanded that "every oblation of thy meat offering shalt thou season with salt; neither shalt thou suffer the salt of the covenant of thy God to be lack-ing from thy meat offering." (Lev. 2:13.) Salt was a token of the covenant that the Lord had made with his people. Jesus perpetuated the symbol by labeling the people themselves as the possessors and promulgators of his covenant. As the salt would season the meat offering, so the disciples of Jesus would season the world and preserve his truth in it.

*"Provide neither gold, nor silver, nor brass in your purses."*
*(Matt. 10:9.)*

Gold, silver, and brass (actually, bronze) were metals used in the Roman period, just as they are today, for commercial barter and for money. They had been used for centuries throughout the Near East in art and architecture, in decoration and attire, and in worship paraphernalia. Gold has always been esteemed as a precious metal, rare in nature and invested with intrinsic usefulness. It must have served a grateful purpose for Joseph and Mary when the infant Jesus received a quantity of gold from the visitors from the east. (See Matt. 2:11.)

Jesus and his disciples had some pointed things to say against the perverted reverence with which people regarded gold and silver and the warped deference to metal objects instead of sacred symbols. "Woe unto you . . . which say, Whosoever shall swear by the temple, it is nothing; but whosoever shall swear by the gold of the temple, he is a debtor! Ye fools and blind: for whether is greater, the gold, or the temple that sanctifieth the gold?" (Matt. 23:16–17.) "Your gold and silver is cankered; and the rust of them shall be a witness against you, and shall eat your flesh as it were fire." (James 5:3.)

"Ye know that ye were not redeemed with corruptible things, as silver and gold." (1 Pet. 1:18.) Instead, what was most important was perseverance in faithful living, the "trial of your faith, being more precious than of gold that perisheth." (1 Pet. 1:7.)

Still, gold could also represent what was immaterial and holy. It could signify the blessings of heaven and the City of God. "I counsel thee to buy of me gold tried in the fire, that thou mayest be rich." (Rev. 3:18.) "[The celestial] city was pure gold, like unto clear glass. . . . And the street of the city was pure gold, as it were transparent glass." (Rev. 21:18, 21.)

The main reference to silver in the Gospels is the thirty pieces of silver given to Judas Iscariot to lead some Jewish leaders to Jesus. (Matt. 26:15.) A great many of the larger denomination Roman and Greek coins were silver, including the oft-mentioned "penny," the King James Translation for *denarius,* a basic Roman coin. (See Matt. 20:2; 22:15–22.) (See "The tables of the moneychangers . . . ," chapter 11.)

It is generally agreed that brass was unknown in Bible times. Though the King James Version uses the word *brass,* actually bronze is intended. Brass is an alloy of copper and zinc (zinc was unknown to the ancients), whereas bronze is an alloy of copper and tin (which was known and used). The Chalcolithic Age [*chalco* = copper] gave way to the Bronze Age, during which the Patriarchs lived. At the time of the Israelite and Philistine incursions into the land, the process of iron smelting became known, and the time period acquired the title "The Iron Age."

The New Testament speaks of bronze vessels (see Mark 7:4; Rev. 18:12) and bronze idols (see Rev. 9:20). Many of the smaller denomination coins were bronze, including the Jewish *lepton,* translated as "mite" in the King James Version. (See Mark 12:41–44.)

Iron was a hard but malleable metal that had already been used for more than a millennium by Jesus' day. New Testament references involve objects made of iron: an iron gate (see Acts 12:10), breastplates of iron (see Rev. 9:9), vessels of iron (see Rev. 18:12), and a rod of iron (see Rev. 2:27; 12:5; 19:15).

# AGRICULTURE, HORTICULTURE, AND VITICULTURE

*"Look on the fields; for they are white already to harvest." (John 4:35.)*

Agriculture is the production of crops in the fields; horticulture, crops in the gardens; and viticulture, grapes in the vineyard. More imagery is drawn from the process and the produce of the fields, gardens, and vineyards than any other source of images in sacred writ. The New Testament attests to every stage of the cycle of agricultural production: plowing, planting or sowing, cultivating, harvesting or reaping, transporting, threshing, sifting, treading, and storing.

We will now follow through the scriptures the *process* and the *produce* of agriculture in New Testament times. We begin with the earth or the soil itself. Two kinds are mentioned: "good ground" and "stony ground." (Mark 4:8, 16.) If ground is too stony for a planting, it may prevent seeds from taking root, so larger stones at least were gathered out of the field and used for building a wall or a fence around the property or perhaps a watchtower.

"He that received seed into the good ground is he that heareth the word, and understandeth it; which also beareth fruit." (Matt. 13:23.) On the other hand, they who received seed into the stony ground, "when they have heard the word, immediately receive it with gladness; and have no root in themselves, and so endure but for a time." (Mark 4:16–17.)

Plowing broke up the soil and furrowed it for the planting. Plowing was likened to the work of God's kingdom, ever progressive, the beginning of the push on to the end, to the bounteous harvest. The Lord responded with such a metaphor to the expressed devotion of two men who asked to be allowed first to resolve other pressing cares. Jesus said, "Follow me. But [one man] said, Lord, suffer me first to go and bury my father. Jesus said unto him, Let the dead bury their dead: but go thou and preach the kingdom of God. And another also said, Lord, I will follow thee; but let me first go bid them farewell, which are at home at my house. And Jesus said unto him, No man, having put his hand to the plough, and looking back, is fit for the kingdom of God." (Luke 9:59–62.)

Jesus' examples of the priority of devotion may seem unusually harsh to us. It's not that those other cares and concerns were to be left undone, but some things are more vital than others; some things are urgent, but others are *important*. This was Jesus' hyperbolic way of describing that, when a man has set his plough on a straight course, when he has planted his life in a more spiritual furrow, he must not look back wistfully on the old life, on the unproductive and fruitless seeds he had formerly sown.

It may not be a simple matter of just *looking* back, either; it may be a problem of *going* back. On another occasion, Jesus illustrated how, when God reveals himself, a man who is on the housetop should not go down into his house to search out and save the old memorabilia, and a man who is "in the field, let him likewise not return back. Remember Lot's wife." (Luke 17:30–32.) There is danger in going back to former conditions, former acquaintances, former ways. The laborer in the field of life should have his eyes set forward, plowing straight lines, ever persevering in a momentum singly dedicated to sowing seeds that will yield a rich harvest.

*"The kingdom of heaven is likened unto a man which sowed good seed in his field." (Matt. 13:24.)*

A favorite and effective way of teaching involved comparing phenomena in nature with the human experience—"I have also spoken by the prophets, and I have multiplied visions, and used similitudes, by the ministry of the prophets." (Hosea 12:10.) A familiar oratorical and literary device of the rabbinic sages during the Roman period was to inquire, "To what shall we liken this?" or "What is he like?" Jesus,

too, adopted this rhetorical device often. "I will liken him unto a wise man . . . [or] a foolish man." (Matt. 7:24–27.) "He is like a man which built an house." (Luke 6:48.)

Sometimes, in asking such a question, Jesus gave many answers: "Unto what is the kingdom of God like? and whereunto shall I resemble it? It is like a grain of mustard seed. . . . Again he said, Whereunto shall I liken the kingdom of God? It is like leaven." (Luke 13:18–21.) "The kingdom of heaven is like unto treasure hid in a field. . . . The kingdom of heaven is like unto a merchant man, seeking goodly pearls. . . . The kingdom of heaven is like unto a net, that was cast into the sea, and gathered of every kind." (Matt. 13:44–47.)

The field was a familiar similitude too: "The field is the world" (Matt. 13:38), and all the people planted in the good field are cultivated and nourished. Eventually comes the harvest. The good produce is gathered into the barn and used to fulfill the measure of its creation, while the bad is cast off.

*"A sower went out to sow his seed." (Luke 8:5.)*

Seeds may represent the word of God: "The seed is the word of God," says Luke. (8:11.) They could also represent the Lord's disciples: Matthew, in another context, wrote that Jesus said, "The good seed are the children of the kingdom." (13:38.)

Whether seed is the word itself or the people who carry the word to all parts of the field (the world), the analogies Jesus made all apply. Some seeds, when sown in the earth, fall by the wayside, where fowls fly in and devour them. Some fall in rocky places, where they are short lived, not sinking roots for nourishment. Some fall among thorns, where they are choked by the weeds of worldliness. Some, however, fall on good ground, where they grow by absorbing the nutrients from sun, soil, and water. (See Matt. 13.)

An important inference is made in these scriptures: the seed itself seems always to be good; the soil in which the seed is planted is what makes the difference. Whether the seed (the word of God) will flourish and become productive depends on what ground it is planted in, whether we are barren, hard, briery, or fertile. Furthermore, if we are fertile, the seed's growth depends on whether we will nourish it by giving it Living Water and exposing it to sufficient Light.

We sometimes call this principle the law of the harvest: "Whatsoever a man soweth, that shall he also reap." (Gal. 6:7.) "He that soweth to his flesh shall of the flesh reap corruption; but he that soweth to the Spirit shall of the Spirit reap life everlasting." (Gal. 6:8.) "He which soweth sparingly shall reap also sparingly; and he which soweth bountifully shall reap also bountifully." (2 Cor. 9:6.)

## "Every plant, which my heavenly Father hath not planted, shall be rooted up." (Matt. 15:13.)

Israelite writers used various literary devices to compare the world of nature to human character and conduct. A *simile* is an explicit comparison, a declaration that one thing is like another. Similes use such words as *like* or *as* to make the comparison. A *metaphor* is an implicit comparison, a declaration that one thing is (or represents) another. *Hypocatastasis* is also a comparison by implication, but the comparison is not actually stated. Unlike similes, the latter two use no words to link comparisons.

Simile: "All flesh is as grass." (1 Pet. 1:24.)
Metaphor: "All flesh is grass." (Isa. 40:6.)
Hypocatastasis: The grass of the field is dry (meaning "people in the world are bereft of Living Water")

Simile: A field is like the world.
Metaphor: "The field is the world." (Matt. 13:38.)
Hypocatastasis: "Look on the fields; for they are white already to harvest." (John 4:35.)

Simile: "Our sons may be as plants grown up." (Ps. 144:12.)
Metaphor: "The men of Judah [are] his pleasant plant." (Isa. 5:7.)
Hypocatastasis: "Every plant, which my heavenly Father hath not planted, shall be rooted up." (Matt. 15:13.)

Figuratively speaking, then, plants are people. God has planted each of his children in the field (the world), and he expects each one to blossom where he or she is planted. The root of a plant is the organ that absorbs and stores what is supplied to the rest of the plant. It is also the means of anchorage. Those who have turned inward and refused God's nutrients, even openly rejecting them, will be rooted up and left without root or branch, which is the ultimate expression of extinction. (See Mal. 4:1; Amos 2:9.)

By the same figure of speech, trees are people. Again, the root of the tree is the essential core, the source and supplier for the body of the tree, which should bear the fruit. "If the root be holy, so are the branches" (Rom. 11:16), but if the root system becomes corrupted, absorbing poisonous elements from its environs, then "the axe is laid unto the root of the trees: every tree therefore which bringeth not forth good fruit is hewn down, and cast into the fire" (Luke 3:9).

As a seed springs up and grows (see Mark 4:27), it needs moisture, which it can receive during the one half of the year by rain and during the other half of the year by dew. "I will give you the rain of your land in his due season, the first rain and the latter rain" (Deut. 11:14), and the "heavens shall drop down dew" (Deut. 33:28; see also Zech. 8:12). Fertilization of the seed is accomplished with dung: "I shall dig about it, and dung it." (Luke 13:8.) Once the sprouts appear, various dangers await them. If it is wartime, the field could be overrun by besieging armies. If time of drought, the tender plant could die from lack of water. If swarms of pests invade the land, the plant could be eaten or contract a disease. Pestilences were often included in catalogs of human catastrophes: earthquakes, famines, and pestilences. (See Matt. 24:7; Luke 21:11.)

*"The harvest truly is plenteous, but the labourers are few." (Matt. 9:37.)*

"Pray ye therefore the Lord of the harvest, that he will send forth labourers into his harvest." (Matt. 9:38.) At the time of harvest, labourers were called to reap the fields, and they were paid according to their labor: "Call the labourers, and give them their hire." (Matt. 20:8.) "He that reapeth receiveth wages, and gathereth fruit unto life eternal." (John 4:36.) The verse from John defines what kind of wages the labourer of God is working for — fruit leading to eternal life.

The harvest, however, is not the climax of a unilateral process. Rather, it is a team effort: "Herein is that saying true, One soweth, and another reapeth. I sent you to reap that whereon ye bestowed no labour: other men laboured, and ye are entered into their labours." (John 4:37–38.) There can be no boastful presumption of singlehandedness in a harvest — many hands brought it to fruition. Even with the labor that human hands can invest in the production process, in the end God is the one who puts the miracle together to consummate the harvest. Paul wrote: "I have planted, Apollos watered; but God gave the increase. So then neither is he that planteth any thing, neither he that watereth; but God that giveth the increase. Now he that planteth and he that watereth are one: and every man shall receive his own reward according to his own labour. For we are labourers together with God." (1 Cor. 3:6–9.)

The full cycle of agricultural production is described in the book of Mark: "So is the kingdom of God, as if a man should cast seed into the ground; and should sleep, and rise night and day, and the seed should spring and grow up, he knoweth not how. For the earth bringeth forth fruit of herself; first the blade, then the ear, after that the full corn in the ear. But when the fruit is brought forth, immediately he putteth in the sickle, because the harvest is come." (Mark 4:26–29.)

This passage from Mark describes in agricultural terminology the plan of God's work on earth. The sower was the Son of God, planting the children of God in the earth. He gave them nourishment, sending the Sun of Righteousness and the Water of Life to bring them to spiritual maturity. When the children of God are ripe, in righteous living or rebellion, he sends his messengers to reap the harvest, that is, to cut off their mortality and bring them to the scales of judgment. The ultimate harvest is "the end of the world." (Matt. 13:39.)

Mortal man also individually prepares for a harvest, the results of all the seeds he has sown in life, showing forth an abundance—we hope—of good works. "Be patient therefore. . . . The husbandman waiteth for the precious fruit of the earth, and hath long patience for it." (James 5:7.) "Let us not be weary in well doing: for in due season we shall reap, if we faint not." (Gal. 6:9.)

*"Thrust in thy sickle . . . ; for the harvest of the earth is ripe." (Rev. 14:15.)*

A sickle was generally a crescent-shaped, sharpened metal tool held in one hand while the other hand clutched some stalks of grain. With one sweep of the arm, the reaper cut the grain and, after gathering many stalks, bound them together into a bundle. Bundles (or sheaves) were spread out to dry on a flat threshing floor usually made of stone, and then stalks (straw), husks, and heads of grain were shredded by animals treading over them, sometimes pulling a threshing sledge (upturned on one end, with jagged pieces of metal or stone fixed with pitch into the bottom—see Amos 1:3).

Following the threshing was the winnowing, which separated the grain from the husks. With a winnowing fork (sometimes called a "fan"), the threshed mixture was tossed into the air, and the afternoon and evening breeze coming off the Mediterranean during the harvest time would carry the lighter husks (the chaff) to settle in their own pile while the heavier grain fell into a pile immediately below the winnower. Any stones or impurities could be further sifted out with a sieve (see Luke 22:31), and then the grain was ready to be used or transported to storage.

The separation of the grain from the impurities is a scenario similar to that envisioned by John the Baptist, where he described the coming Messiah as one "whose fan [winnowing fork] is in his hand, and he will throughly purge his floor, and gather his wheat into the garner; but he will burn up the chaff with unquenchable fire." (Matt. 3:12; see Luke 3:17.)

*"Two women shall be grinding at the mill." (Matt. 24:41.)*

Once grain is threshed, winnowed, and sifted, it is ready to be used or stored. It may be taken directly to the mill for grinding into flour. One type of mill in the Roman period was made from local lime-

*Top left:* Along the shore of the Sea of Galilee, seeds fall among stones, thorns, and good soil. *Top right:* Basalt grinding mills found at Capernaum. *Center left:* Bottom side of a threshing sledge. *Center right:* Winnowing—separating the wheat from chaff. *Bottom left:* Fields of wheat growing in Galilee. *Bottom right:* Ancient olive oil lamp.

stone or basalt, with one conical piece serving as a base over which an hourglass-shaped stone was placed. Grain was dropped into the top, to be ground to fine powder by one or two persons (or an animal) pushing a wooden post attached to the sides.

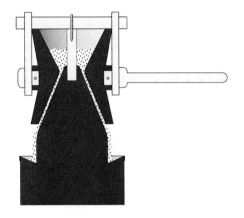

Millstones were extremely heavy, which accounts for their illustrative use in Jesus' teaching: "Whoso shall offend one of these little ones which believe in me, it were better for him that a millstone were hanged about his neck, and that he were drowned in the depth of the sea." (Matt. 18:6.)

In describing the destruction of the wicked at the Messiah's coming in the end of days, Jesus indicated that two would be working in the field; one would be taken and the other left. Two women would be grinding at the mill; one would be taken and the other left. (See Matt. 24:40–41.) In such a selective destruction, which is the preferred situation: to be taken or to be left? Malachi posed these questions to Israel: "Who may abide the day of his coming? and who shall stand when he appeareth?" (Mal. 3:2.)

The one who is taken may be understood as the one who is rescued, preserved, taken up to join the Lord when he "cometh with ten thousands of his saints" (Jude 1:14), and the other is left to face doom and annihilation. On the other hand, the opposite is a viable interpretation: the one is taken—that is, caught in the holocaust and destroyed—whereas the other is left, or spared, kept safe from the surrounding consumption. Regardless of the interpretation, the point is the same as the analogy of wheat and chaff—some are good and some are bad; some are saved for further use, while others have to be rejected and discarded.

We have seen how the Messiah will come with fan in hand to purge the threshing floor and gather his wheat into the garner. (See Matt. 3:12.) The word translated "garner" is *apotheke* in Greek, a storehouse or barn used as a granary. "In the time of harvest I will say to the reapers, Gather ye together first the tares, and bind them in bundles to burn them: but gather the wheat into my barn." (Matt. 13:30.) "Consider the ravens: for they neither sow nor reap; which neither have storehouse nor barn; and God feedeth them." (Luke 12:24.)

*"Ye shall know them by their fruits." (Matt. 7:16.)*

Having examined the process of agricultural production, we may now look more closely at the produce itself. Not surprisingly, we find the words and works of men and women compared to fruit, good works being good fruit and evil works being bad fruit. Whether in the

81

world of plant life or human life, God wants good produce, good fruit. "Bring forth therefore fruits worthy of repentance." (Luke 3:8.) "Let ours also learn to maintain good works for necessary uses, that they be not unfruitful." (Titus 3:14.) When we compare life with planting and nourishing seeds, which lead to an abundant harvest, we plainly and clearly understand the expectation of Deity: "When the time of the fruit drew near, he sent his servants . . . that they might receive the fruits of it." (Matt. 21:34.)

If a people is unproductive, refusing to labor for the rich harvest, as the Lord has said, "The kingdom of God shall be taken from you, and given to a nation bringing forth the fruits thereof." (Matt. 21:43.) "I have chosen you, and ordained you, that ye should go and bring forth fruit, and that your fruit should remain." (John 15:16.)

The fruit is obviously not perishable earthly fruit but "fruit that remains," or endures on into the eternal world: "He that reapeth receiveth wages, and gathereth fruit unto life eternal." (John 4:36.) Paul also said on many occasions that he was laboring for that lasting fruit among the various peoples of his missionary journeys: "I purposed to come unto you . . . that I might have some fruit among you also, even as among other Gentiles." (Rom. 1:13.)

Paul taught that "we should bring forth fruit unto God" (Rom. 7:4), and he labeled and defined what some of the fruits should be: "The fruit of the Spirit is love, joy, peace, longsuffering, gentleness, goodness, faith" (Gal. 5:22). He wrote about "the fruits of righteousness" and "the fruit of my labour" (Philip. 1:11, 22), "the peaceable fruit of righteousness" and "the fruit of our lips" (Heb. 12:11; 13:15), meaning good works and words.

Some of the main fruits of the land, grown either in the fields or gardens or vineyards, by which the prophets and Jesus illustrated the lessons of eternal life, are wheat, barley, olives, figs, and grapes (discussed in the viticulture section, pp. 93–95). These are five of the seven fruits of the land of promise mentioned in Deuteronomy 8:8 (the other two are pomegranates and honey, actually the syrup of dates), all of which flower between Passover and Shavuot (the Feast of Weeks, or Pentecost), generally between April and June.

*"Except a corn of wheat fall into the ground and die, it abideth alone."*
*(John 12:24.)*

To Americans, corn is a specific crop featuring a cob that grows on a stalk. The King James Version uses the British word *corn* generally for grain of all kinds. Actually three different Greek words are translated as "corn" in the New Testament: *sporimos,* referring to a planted field; *sitos,* grain, especially wheat; and *stachus,* a head, or ear, of grain. The reason, therefore, that *corn* and *wheat* are both used in the above passage from John is that corn can mean the head of grain, whichever grain it may be, and wheat is specifically the kernels of wheat.

The scripture indicates that an ear of wheat must be planted in the ground and "die"; that is, it must change from its present structure to become something bigger and better, to become fruitful. Jesus used this analogy from nature to foreshadow his own death, "The hour is come, that the Son of man should be glorified. . . . If it [a corn of wheat] die, it bringeth forth much fruit." (John 12:23–24.) Sacrifice is what engenders the blessings of eternal life. Burying the carnal man is necessary in order to give birth to the spiritual man.

Grain harvest happened each year between Passover and Shavuot, in the first month or month and a half of the warm season. Barley was harvested first, at the end of April, and wheat a month later, at the end of May or beginning of June. Shavuot, then, was a harvest festival. As the Lord told Israel, "Thou shalt keep . . . the feast of harvest, the firstfruits of thy labours, which thou hast sown in the field." (Ex. 23:15–16.)

After Jesus' encounter with the Samaritan woman at Jacob's Well, his disciples returned with food, and Jesus used the meal as a setting for a lesson, a teaching moment: "I have meat [food] to eat that ye know not of. . . . Say not ye, There are yet four months, and then cometh harvest? behold, I say unto you, Lift up your eyes, and look on the fields; for they are white already to harvest." (John 4:31–35.)

To this day, many of the fields along the road leading to Jacob's Well at ancient Shechem are planted with wheat. If there were yet four months to the harvest, Jesus must have journeyed through Samaria in late December or early January. Calling on his disciples to look out on the whitened fields ready to harvest was his way of sug-

gesting that the harvest of humanity was ripe all around them, even among the Samaritans, and that they could thrust in their sickles and reap fruit leading to eternal life. (See John 4:36.) The succeeding verses indicate that Jesus and his disciples did labor among the Samaritans, and many of them believed in him.

The most famous use of wheat in Jesus' teachings was that expressed in his parable of the wheat and the tares, recorded only in Matthew 13 and interpreted by the Lord over eighteen hundred years later in Doctrine and Covenants 18:1–7. "The kingdom of heaven is likened unto a man which sowed good seed in his field: but while men slept, his enemy came and sowed tares among the wheat." (Matt. 13:24–25.)

The word *tares* occurs in the New Testament only in the one parable. The Greek word *zizanion,* translated as "tares," allegedly comes from a Semitic root and refers to weeds in grain. Most assume it is the somewhat poisonous bearded darnel, or weed grass. It resembles wheat in its early stages of growth, and the roots of the two are often intertwined. (See Matt. 13:29.) The owner of the wheat field discouraged those who wanted to go in immediately to weed the crop, "Lest while ye gather up the tares, ye root up also the wheat with them. Let both grow together until the harvest: and in the time of harvest I will say to the reapers, Gather ye together first the tares, and bind them in bundles to burn them: but gather the wheat into my barn." (Vv. 29–30.)

The apostles were the sowers of the good seed, but Satan sowed the bad seed.

(See D&C 86:2–3.) The tares represent apostates, flourishing together with the righteous (the wheat) in the Lord's kingdom. At judgment time, however, there would be a separation between them, as with the wheat and chaff. (See D&C 86:7.)

Though mentioned often in the Old Testament, barley is mentioned but once in the Gospels, in connection with Jesus' ministry on the northern shores of the Sea of Galilee. People flocked to hear him teach, and on one occasion the apostles became nervous about how such multitudes would find sufficient food to eat. Andrew underscored their predicament by informing Jesus that "there is a lad here, which hath five barley loaves, and two small fishes: but what are they among so many?" (John 6:9.)

Andrew's information demonstrated the bewilderment the apostles felt; he emphasized that there were two *small* fishes and five *barley* loaves. All four Gospel writers recorded this incident, but John is the only one who specifically mentioned what the loaves were made of. Barley was a staple grain for the poorer people, less favored than wheat. Fishes that were small and loaves that were made of barley would supply meager nourishment to few people.

Bread was the basic stuff of life. "Give us this day our daily bread" (Matt. 6:11) was the life-long plea of a people dependent on the rain of heaven and the produce of the land. To "eat bread" or "break bread" came to be synonymous with "partake of a meal." (See Mark 3:20; 7:2, 5; Luke 14:1, 15; 24:35; John 13:18.) However, the God who granted the water and

fertility warned that the human soul needed more than physical food: "Man shall not live by bread alone, but by every word that proceedeth out of the mouth of God." (Matt. 4:4.)

Unleavened bread (matza) was used during the week-long Feast of Unleavened Bread in connection with the Passover. It commemorated the Exodus from Egypt, when the Israelites had to make unleavened bread because there was not enough time for bread to rise before they left. (See Ex. 12:15; Matt. 26:17; Acts 12:3.)

Leaven is what makes bread rise, and spiritual leaven would cause the kingdom of heaven to rise. (See Matt. 13:13.) Jesus warned his disciples, however, to be careful of the leaven of the Pharisees and Sadducees, that is, of their doctrine. (See Matt. 16:11–12.) Paul adapted his own definition for leaven: "Know ye not that a little leaven leaveneth the whole lump? Purge out therefore the old leaven, that ye may be a new lump. . . . Let us keep the feast, not with old leaven, neither with the leaven of malice and wickedness; but with the unleavened bread of sincerity and truth." (1 Cor. 5:6–8.)

Such an indispensable ingredient of life as bread could not have escaped the attention of biblical writers imbued with an affection for similitudes. Jesus took up the loftiest symbolic use of bread in his discourse in the synagogue at Capernaum: "The bread of God is he which cometh down from heaven, and giveth life unto the world. . . . I am the bread of life: he that cometh to me shall never hunger . . . I am the living bread which came down from heaven: if any man eat of this bread, he shall live for ever: and the bread that I will give is my flesh, which I will give for the life of the world." (John 6:33, 35, 51.)

*"The branches . . . partakest of the root and fatness of the olive tree." (Rom. 11:17.)*

Surprisingly, the word *olives* occurs eleven times in the Gospels, all of them referring to the Mount of Olives (where olive trees grew in antiquity and still grow today). Jesus Christ and his apostles did not mention the olive tree, however, except by indirectly referring to the tree through its product, olive oil.

The olive tree had occupied first place in agriculture throughout Israel's history to the time of Jesus, and it even provided one of the country's designations: a land of olive oil. (See Deut. 8:8.) It thrives well in the hill country and needs no irrigation. It can endure long periods of drought, and little care is needed until the harvest. The upper side of the olive leaf is dark green, while the underside is covered with miniature whitish scales, giving it a silvery sheen. "Israel was called 'an olive tree leafy and fair' [see Jer. 11:16] because they [Israel] shed light on all."[1]

Olive oil was used anciently for culinary, cosmetic, funerary, medicinal, and ritual purposes. Its most important use, though, was to provide light. It provides the clearest, brightest, and steadiest flame of all the vegetable oils. In one of Jesus' last recorded parables, he described a procession of young women (members of God's kingdom) going out to meet the bridegroom (the Messiah). Lamps were re-

quired for brilliancy and beauty. The oil for the lamps was symbolic of spiritual preparation on the part of the members of his kingdom, those who desire to participate in the marriage feast, which symbolizes his coming in glory:

"The kingdom of heaven [is] likened unto ten virgins, which took their lamps, and went forth to meet the bridegroom. And five of them were wise, and five were foolish. They that were foolish took their lamps, and took no oil with them: but the wise took oil in their vessels with their lamps. . . . [When the bridegroom came,] all those virgins arose, and trimmed [prepared] their lamps. And the foolish said unto the wise, Give us of your oil; for our lamps are gone out. But the wise answered, saying, Not so; lest there be not enough for us and you: but go ye rather to them that sell, and buy for yourselves. And while they went to buy, the bridegroom came; and they that were ready went in with him to the marriage: and the door was shut." (Matt. 25:1–8.)

In early Israelite history, olive oil was used for sacred functions. Objects and persons set apart for the work of God, such as prophets, priests, and kings, were anointed with consecrated oil. With the Messiah (Hebrew, *mashiah,* meaning "anointed one"), the roles of prophet, priest, and king come together. Jesus, citing a messianic prophecy in Isaiah (see 61:1), told those attending the synagogue in Nazareth, "The Spirit of the Lord is upon me, because he hath anointed me to preach" (Luke 4:18).

Another messianic prophecy from Isaiah involves the olive tree. The perpetuity of the House of Jesse is illustrated with a dramatic metaphor from the fields of Israel: "There shall come forth a rod out of the stem of Jesse, and a Branch shall grow out of his roots"; or, as the parallelism translates directly from the Hebrew, "There shall come forth a branch [*khoter*] out of the trunk of Jesse: indeed, a shoot [*netzer*] from his roots shall bear fruit." (11:1.)

Matthew may have referred to this prophecy when he saw in Jesus the fulfillment of what was spoken by the prophets, "He shall be called a Nazarene [in Hebrew, *notzri*, the same root word used by Isaiah and variously translated "Branch" or "shoot"]." (Matt. 2:23.) The terms *khoter* and *netzer* can be used interchangeably, though in this case *khoter* is a branch or shoot from the trunk of the tree, whereas *netzer* is a shoot from the root system, and only a shoot or branch from the root can start new life. The olive tree is the only tree that can have apparently dead branches and even a trunk and still produce, sometime later, new life from the root. Characteristics of the olive tree are called to bear witness that the Messiah, a descendant of David, son of Jesse, would grow from the original root of the family tree of the royal house of David.

Extending certain courtesies to an honored guest, like washing the feet, giving a kiss of greeting, and anointing the head with oil, was customary among the Jews in New Testament times. Jesus chastised the host of a dinner by contrasting the host's lack of courtesies with the courtesies given him by a sinful woman: "He turned to the woman, and said unto Si-mon, Seest thou this woman? I entered into thine house, thou gavest me no water for my feet: but she hath washed my feet with tears. . . . Thou gavest me no kiss: but this woman since the time I came in hath not ceased to kiss my feet. My head with oil thou didst not anoint: but this woman hath anointed my feet with ointment." (Luke 7:44–46.)

The use of olive oil for medicinal purposes is illustrated in the parable of the good Samaritan. The Samaritan bound up the wounds of the assaulted Jew, "pouring in oil and wine." (Luke 10:34.) Oil and wine were believed to have curative and antiseptic properties, as rabbinical sources of the time also attest.

As the priests who ministered in the Temple used olive oil as part of their ritual offerings, so those ministering in the early Christian Church used it to anoint and to heal. The apostles were sent out to teach throughout the land, "and they cast out many devils, and anointed with oil many that were sick, and healed them." (Mark 6:13.) Leaders of the early Church encouraged the members to use olive oil in administering to the sick: "Is any sick among you? let him call for the elders of the church; and let them pray over him, anointing him with oil." (James 5:14.)

*"I come seeking fruit on this fig tree, and find none." (Luke 13:7.)*

A practical lesson from nature was taught at the end of each winter season: the fig tree was a harbinger of hot weather, a signal of summertime. The writer of the most exquisite pastoral love poetry in the Bible observed, "The winter is past, the

*Top left:* An ancient olive tree in the Garden of Gethsemane on the Mount of Olives. *Top right:* Leaves and fruit of the olive tree. *Center left:* New branches coming out of the roots of the olive tree. (See Isa. 11:1.) *Center right:* Leaves and fruit of the fig tree. *Bottom left:* Sign at the entrance of the Garden of Gethsemane. *Bottom right:* Tiny mustard seeds held in the palm of a hand for size comparison.

rain is over and gone; the flowers appear on the earth. . . . The fig tree putteth forth her green figs." (Song. 2:11–13.) Jesus made a similar observation from nature: "When [the fig tree's] branch is yet tender, and putteth forth leaves, ye know that summer is nigh." (Matt. 24:32.)

The fig tree and the vine together were tokens or types of prosperity and secure living. From former Hebrew literature, we have the following examples: "Judah and Israel dwelt safely, every man under his vine and under his fig tree, from Dan even to Beer-sheba." (1 Kgs. 4:25.) Assyrian officers harrassing Jerusalemites in the days of Hezekiah said, "Thus saith the king of Assyria, Make an agreement with me by a present, and come out to me: and eat ye every one of his vine, and every one of his fig tree." (Isa. 36:16.)

This combination was also featured prominently in prophecies of destruction or prosperity: "Lo, I will bring a nation upon you from far, O house of Israel, saith the Lord: it is a mighty nation, it is an ancient nation, a nation whose language thou knowest not. . . . They shall eat up thy vines and thy fig trees." (Jer. 5:15–17.) "Fear not, O land; be glad and rejoice: for the Lord will do great things. . . . For the tree beareth her fruit, the fig tree and the vine do yield their strength." (Joel 2:21–22.) "In that day, saith the Lord of hosts, shall ye call every man his neighbour under the vine and under the fig tree." (Zech. 3:10.)

"Every man under his vine and under his fig tree" became a figurative and formulaic expression of living comfortably, safely, and securely. Just after Philip had encouraged his friend Nathanael to come and meet Jesus of Nazareth, Nathanael remarked, "Can there any good thing come out of Nazareth?" The following conversation ensued: "Jesus saw Nathanael coming to him, and saith of him, Behold an Israelite indeed, in whom is no guile! Nathanael saith unto him, Whence knowest thou me? Jesus answered and said unto him, Before that Philip called thee, when thou wast under the fig tree, I saw thee." (John 1:45–48.)

The statement may be taken literally—Nathanael may have been meditating under a fig tree. Or the statement may be figurative—"under the fig tree" may mean that Nathanael was living comfortably and contentedly, having no reason to make any changes in his life. By meeting Jesus, however, the course of his life would change abruptly and dramatically. Some rabbinical sources suggest that "under a fig tree" is the proper place for personal scripture study and that the phrase may be idiomatic, synonymous with "in search of truth."

The most memorable encounter with a fig tree in the New Testament occurred during the last week of Jesus' life on earth, while Jesus was walking one morning from Bethany over the Mount of Olives to Jerusalem. As he walked, he became hungry, "and when he saw a fig tree in the way, he came to it, and found nothing thereon, but leaves only, and said unto it, Let no fruit grow on thee henceforward for ever. And presently the fig tree withered away." (Matt. 21:18–19.) Mark added, after Jesus came and found nothing but leaves, "For the time of figs was not yet." (11:13.)

Insight and interpretation may be gleaned from Luke's account, which was set in the form of a parable: "A certain man had a fig tree planted in his vineyard; and he came and sought fruit thereon, and found none. Then said he unto the dresser of his vineyard, Behold, these three years I come seeking fruit on this fig tree, and find none: cut it down; why cumbereth it the ground? And he answering said unto him, Lord, let it alone this year also, till I shall dig about it, and dung it: And if it bear fruit, well: and if not, then after that thou shalt cut it down." (Luke 13:6–9.)

The fig tree was common in rabbinical lore as a symbol or type of the nation of Israel. Jesus too adopted the symbolism in this incident and parable. We have no other instance of Jesus using his divine power to destroy, but he deemed the life of the fig tree a necessary teaching tool, to illustrate in an unforgettable way the religious history of Israel. The fig tree, or the people of Israel, had been planted in the part of God's vineyard that was the land of Israel. The tree had been watered and nourished by the Lord of the vineyard through his earthly husbandmen. It had been pruned by centuries of adversity, and it had been expected to bear fruit.

Since it was Passover time in Jerusalem, half a year before figs would normally ripen, Jesus must have been referring to previous years' unfruitfulness. From Jesus' point of view, this tree had produced a showy flush of leaves but was perennially barren and fruitless—"these three years I come seeking fruit on this fig tree, and find none." Judaism at the time of Jesus was ripe in ritualism and regimentation. It had been aggressive in maintaining the finer points of the law of Moses and the traditions, but it had neglected the weightier matters of justice, mercy, and faith. The fig tree representing Israel had not been cut down in that generation, but because it still bore no fruit after another season or generation of growth, it was removed, and pieces of it were scattered to other parts of the vineyard.

*"Smoking flax shall he not quench."*
*(Matt. 12:20.)*

Early Christians saw in Jesus the fulfillment of Isaiah's visions of the Suffering Servant. Isaiah 42 begins with the prophet speaking messianically, describing him as the epitome of gentle tenderness, unwilling to harm even the weakest plant. "A bruised reed shall he not break, and the smoking flax shall he not quench." (V. 3; see Matt. 12:20.)

The Greek word for flax was *linen,* which is one of the products prepared from the fibrous plant. Flax was grown in various parts of the Near East anciently, especially in Egypt. It was cultivated in the tropical climate of Jericho at the time of the Israelites' incursion into the land of Canaan. (See Josh. 2:6.) The "smoking flax" is a reference to the wick of an oil lamp. The gentleness of the Messiah would figuratively disallow his even putting out the smoking linen wick used in a lamp.

The New Testament speaks of "clean linen cloth" (Matt. 27:59), "fine linen" (Mark 15:46; Luke 16:19), and "pure and white linen" (Rev. 15:6). Linen was used as burial cloth for the dead; most New

Testament references to linen refer to the shroud or burial cloth of Jesus: "When Joseph had taken the body, he wrapped it in a clean linen cloth." (Matt. 27:59.) "Then took they the body of Jesus, and wound it in linen clothes with the spices, as the manner of the Jews is to bury." (John 19:40.)

*"In the place where he was crucified there was a garden." (John 19:41.)*

Having examined the process and produce of agriculture in the fields of the land of Jesus, we now turn to the science and art of horticulture (Latin, *hortus,* meaning "garden"), which is the growing of fruits, vegetables, flowers, and ornamental plants in gardens.

Scriptural history begins in the Garden of Eden, or the Garden of God, as Ezekiel called it. The Old Testament speaks of gardens of herbs, the king's garden, and palace gardens, and uses the simile of progress and prosperity, "like a watered garden." (Isa. 58:11.) In the New Testament, we find one lone reference to seeds planted in a garden (see Luke 13:19) and two references to gardens in Jerusalem: the Garden of Gethsemane (see John 18:1, 26) and a garden where Jesus' body was laid in the borrowed sepulchre of a friend (see John 19:41; 20:15).

*"Ye tithe mint and rue" (Luke 11:42); "ye pay tithe of . . . anise and cummin" (Matt. 23:23).*

Herbs are plants grown for flavoring, for aroma, or for medicinal value. Paul identified in his writings one of these values: "One believeth that he may eat all things: another, who is weak, eateth herbs." (Rom. 14:2.) Mustard, mint, and rue are specifically noted as garden herbs.

Mint, rue (Latin, *Ruta graveolens*), anise (Greek, *anethon*) or dill, and cummin were all pungent or aromatic garden herbs with culinary and medicinal value. The Pharisaic tithe on these insignificant and inexpensive plants symbolized the painstaking adherence to fine points of the law, at the same time omitting "the weightier matters of the law, judgment, mercy, and faith." Jesus told the Pharisees, "These ought ye to have done, and not to leave the other undone." (Matt. 23:23.) Jesus observed that the Pharisees tithed "all manner of herbs" while passing over "judgment and the love of God." (Luke 11:42.)

*"The kingdom of heaven is like to a grain of mustard seed." (Matt. 13:31.)*

There is only partial consensus among botanists who have studied biblical plants as to which member of the mustard family represented in the land of Israel could be the "tree" Jesus referred to. The most likely candidate is *Brassica nigra,* from which the important condiment black mustard is derived. Although rabbinical writings label mustard as a field plant, it was also planted in gardens.

As with most Semites, Jesus loved a contrast, even a hyperbolic contrast, to teach a lesson. Though the land of Israel itself, and the villages of Bethlehem and Nazareth, were all small and relatively insignificant, yet, as New Testament writers understood, out of them would come the

90

Messiah, the King of all the earth. Thus the mustard seed is an apt analogy: it "is less than all the seeds that be in the earth" (Mark 4:31), "which a man took, and cast into his garden; and it grew, and waxed a great tree; and the fowls of the air lodged in the branches of it" (Luke 13:19).

Although the mustard seed is not really the smallest of all seeds, proverbially or hyperbolically it denotes the strength and power inherent in even the smallest particle. "If ye have faith as a grain of mustard seed, ye shall say unto this mountain, Remove hence to yonder place; and it shall remove; and nothing shall be impossible unto you." (Matt. 17:20.)

Jesus also taught that the kingdom he was establishing was like a mustard seed, "which indeed is the least of all seeds: but when it is grown, it is the greatest among herbs." (Matt. 13:32.) That the glorious kingdom of God would begin in such a small and obscure way was a very un-Jewish teaching; that the kingdom would be even "the least" of all kingdoms was near heresy. Most Jews in the days of Jesus expected the Messiah to come and champion their cause, overthrow the Romans (as Judah the Maccabee had overthrown the Greeks), and reestablish a mighty kingdom of the Jews with the Anointed One ruling as King. Jesus, however, implanted a different concept of greatness arising out of something small.

*"And brought a mixture of myrrh and aloes . . . " (John 19:39.)*

For a discussion of myrrh and aloes, see "They returned, and prepared spices and ointments," chapter 10.

*"They filled a spunge with vinegar, and put it upon hyssop, and put it to his mouth." (John 19:29.)*

The hyssop (Hebrew, *ezov;* Arabic, *za'atar*) is a small tree (though we might call it a shrub or a bush). It is used as a food, spice, and medicine, and the woody stem and branches are often used for kindling. Its appearance is unimposing and unpretentious, and it was used in contrast to the lofty and mighty cedar. Solomon "spake of trees, from the cedar tree that is in Lebanon even unto the hyssop that springeth out of the wall." (1 Kgs. 4:33.)

The cedar represented pride and haughtiness, whereas the hyssop symbolized modesty, humility, and purity. Leviticus 14 details its use in the cleansing process for a leper. A hyssop branch was also used in applying blood to the doorposts of Israelite houses on the night that the angel of death passed over (see Ex. 12:21–23); later, Moses used hyssop in sprinkling the blood of the testament on the scriptures and on the people (see Ex. 24:6–8; Heb. 9:19–20). David, aching to be cleansed, pleaded, "Purge me with hyssop, and I shall be clean." (Ps. 51:7.)

The scripture subhead recalls the scene of a crucified Jesus hanging on the cross and crying out that he was thirsty, his only spoken expression of physical suffering. Some soldiers attending him lifted a vinegar-filled sponge to his lips on a hyssop branch. The vinegar was a kind of cheap, sour wine commonly drunk by poorer people and soldiers. Use of the hyssop branch may have some symbolic relation to the saving blood spread on the houses

*Top left:* The lowly hyssop — symbol of humility and purity. *Top right:* The hyssop bush contrasted with the mighty cedar behind it. *Center left:* Grapes on the vine — one of the seven species of the promised land identified in Deuteronomy 8:8. *Center right:* Wine "bottles" made from goatskins. *Bottom left:* A stone tower to watch over the vineyard. *Bottom right:* A vineyard with piles of branches cut off and ready to be burned.

of Israel during that first Passover night, or to the blood of remission that Moses applied to the people. Paul noted that the Mosaic practices were "patterns," "figures," "shadows," and "images" of things to come. (See Heb. 9–10.) Or it may have been a symbol of humility involved in the fulfillment of a messianic prophecy: "In my thirst they gave me vinegar to drink." (Ps. 69:21.)

*"Gather the clusters of the vine of the earth; for her grapes are fully ripe." (Rev. 14:18.)*

In addition to the produce of field and garden, we find in the New Testament the familiar motif of vineyard and vine. Viticulture became a prominent occupation for the settling Israelites. It also figured significantly in Bible symbolism and imagery. From Jesus' parables, we learn much about viticulture in New Testament times.

The owner, or "lord of the vineyard," employed several types of workers: the steward or manager (see Matt. 20:8), the vinedresser (see Luke 13:7) or husbandman (Greek, *georgos,* meaning "farmer" or "worker of the land"—see Matt. 21:33), the laborer or temporary worker hired from the marketplace (see Matt. 20:1–16), and the watchman (see Matt. 21:33).

"Hear another parable: There was a certain householder, which planted a vineyard, and hedged it round about, and digged a winepress in it, and built a tower, and let it out to husbandmen, and went into a far country." (Matt. 21:33.) The householder let his vineyard out; that is, he leased it to husbandmen, evidence of

tenant farming in vineyards. The husbandman is characterized as being patient in waiting for the fruit to come (see James 5:7), and he was to be the first partaker of the fruit (see 2 Tim. 2:6).

A typical vineyard included a hedge: a fence or enclosure, usually consisting of thorn bushes or loose stone walls (from stones gathered out of the rocky soil to make it more cultivable). It also included a winepress and winevat (sometimes spelled winefat). The press was normally a stone trough with a hole in the bottom or side through which the grape juice would flow into a vat or container below.

Grapes could be pressed by treading on them (see Rev. 14:20; 19:15) or by crushing them with heavy stones. Juice was extracted from the vat and put into wineskins ("bottles" made from goatskins) or earthenware jars. New wine—grape juice—was put into new bottles, "else the new wine doth burst the [old] bottles, and the wine is spilled." (Mark 2:22.) Fermenting wine would expand and stretch the wineskin and cause it to burst if it was old and already stretched. Jesus' intent was to avoid packaging the fresh, new fruit of the vine (the gospel produced from the True Vine) in the old and already stretched skin of Judaism. With pointed insight into human nature, he explained that "no man . . . having drunk old wine straightway desireth new: for he saith, The old is better." (Luke 5:39.)

A tower was built of stones, not only to reclaim the rocky soil to more easily facilitate its cultivation, but also to guard and protect the vineyard. It offered an elevated position from which the watchman could see approaching danger (for example, thieves). The vineyard was especially guarded in the harvest season. The tower also served as a temporary dwelling and shelter from sun to avoid heat load and dehydration and was a place of storage for the fresh fruit. Remains of thousands of these towers may still be seen in the hill country of Judaea and Samaria.

Vines were planted abundantly in the hill regions, especially around Hebron, places less suited for cultivation of grains. Vines demanded particular attention to keep them fruitful. They were pruned (see John 15:2) in the spring, and the withered branches were "cast . . . into the fire, and they are burned" (John 15:6). Not only grapevines but also olive trees and fig trees (see Luke 13:6) could be found in many vineyards.

One of Jesus' most poignant applications of nature to the religious history of Israel is his parable recorded in Luke 20, where God himself is the lord of the vineyard, sending his servants and eventually even his own Son, to gather fruit in the vineyard. In the perspective of the early Christian disciples, the Lord of the vineyard had sent his servants the prophets and even his Son, all of whom were rejected and killed, and the unproductive vineyard was then given over to others for a long season:

"A certain man planted a vineyard, and let it forth to husbandmen, and went into a far country for a long time. And at the season he sent a servant to the husbandmen, that they should give him of the fruit of the vineyard: but the husbandmen beat him, and sent him away empty. And again he sent another servant: and they beat him also, and entreated him shamefully, and sent him away empty. And again he sent a third: and they wounded him also, and cast him out.

"Then said the lord of the vineyard, What shall I do: I will send my beloved son: it may be they will reverence him when they see him. But when the husbandmen saw him, they reasoned among themselves, saying, This is the heir: come, let us kill him, that the inheritance may be ours. So they cast him out of the vineyard, and killed him. What therefore shall the lord of the vineyard do unto them? He shall come and destroy these husbandmen, and shall give the vineyard to others." (Vv. 9–16.)

One of the most brilliant and profound outpourings of imagery in all the world's literature is that recorded by John, where Jesus called himself metaphorically the "true vine." The analogy manifests perfect detail of viticulture and of the spiritual life:

"I am the true vine, and my Father is the husbandman. Every branch in me that beareth not fruit he taketh away: and every branch that beareth fruit, he purgeth [pruneth] it, that it may bring forth more fruit. . . . Abide in me, and I in you. As the branch cannot bear fruit of itself, except it abide in the vine; no more can ye, except ye abide in me. I am the vine, ye are the branches: He that abideth in me, and I in him, the same bringeth forth much fruit: for without me ye can do nothing. If a man abide not in me, he is cast forth as a branch, and is withered; and men gather them, and cast them into the fire, and they are burned. . . . Herein is my

Father glorified, that ye bear much fruit; so shall ye be my disciples." (John 15: 1–8.)

Only the branch that stays firmly connected to the Vine and its roots can drink deeply of the Water of Life and absorb the Sun of Righteousness and all other necessary nutrients to assure growth leading to fruitfulness. Despite the prunings (or trials of life) when the branch is cut down (or humbled), or actually *because of* such prunings, the branch can be made more fruitful. Those who remain unproductive in the end will be cut off and burned in the fire.

## NOTE

1. Midrash, *Shmot Raba*, 36, 1.

# NATURAL VEGETATION

*"Every good tree bringeth forth good fruit." (Matt. 7:17.)*

Trees have always been a significant feature of the landscape of Israel. They have, therefore, figured prominently in the physical survival of the people and in the didactic imagery of their preachers and writers. There are more references to the fig tree in the New Testament than any other tree, but the mustard tree (see Luke 13:19), the sycamine (see Luke 17:6), the sycomore (see Luke 19:4), the palm (see John 12:13), the olive (see Rom. 11:17, 24), and the "tree of life" (see Rev. 2:7) are also mentioned.

In the Near East, trees provided life support in the form of food stuffs and material for buildings, shelter, occupational tools, and implements; and they were used for shade and for prevention of landscape deterioration. Because of their quintessential role, trees in the biblical periods enjoyed a careful respect and near reverence from the inhabitants of the Holy Land.

Trees were among the favorite objects of biblical imagery and symbolism. Comparing the characteristics of trees to the human experience was a familiar teaching approach among the Jewish sages for centuries. Following is an example from the most known and used part of the Mishnah. One rabbi used to say, "One whose wisdom is greater than his deeds, what is he like? A tree whose branches are many and its roots few. And the wind comes and roots it up and overturns it on its face. But one whose deeds exceed his wisdom, what is he like? A tree whose branches are few and its roots many; so that even if all the winds that are in the world come and blow upon it they stir it not from its place."[1]

From Jesus and his disciples come the following examples of trees as object lessons. Trees represent people. "Even so every good tree bringeth forth good fruit; but a corrupt tree bringeth forth evil fruit. Every tree that bringeth not forth good fruit is hewn down, and cast into the fire. . . . Either make the tree good, and his fruit good; or else make the tree corrupt, and his fruit corrupt: for the tree is known by his fruit." (Matt. 7:17, 19; 12:33.)

Portending ominous consequences for the future of his people, Jesus queried, "If they do these things in a green tree, what shall be done in the dry?" (Luke 23:31.)

Such was the contemporary proverb, meaning in this context that, if such an outrage can be perpetrated in a time of relative tranquility (*pax Romana*), what terrifying and foreboding judgments will be meted out when the calm is dried up and destruction and desolation (see Matt. 24; Luke 21) would be unleashed on the Holy City? Ironically, Peter noted that Jesus himself "they slew and hanged on a tree." (Acts 10:39.)

### "Is not this the carpenter's son?" (Matt. 13:55.)

Geographical and geological evidence suggests that forest was more plentiful in the Holy Land during the Roman period than in any succeeding time until our present century. Wood was available and was used in the construction business during Jesus' day. There are two occurrences in the New Testament of the word *carpenter*, referring to Joseph and Jesus. The above quotation suggests that Jesus' mortal guardian, Joseph, was a carpenter, and Mark renders a similar question, "Is not this the carpenter, the son of Mary?" (6:3), suggesting that Jesus himself was a carpenter also.

But were they really carpenters? The Greek term in these two places is *tekton*, meaning "artificer" or "craftsman." Though contemporary usage in the first century A.D. allows the connection with woodworking, there is little specific indication that Joseph and Jesus were carpenters, workers of wood. Matthew and Luke record only one reference to the processes of carpentry in Jesus' teachings: "Why beholdest thou the mote [speck or splinter] that is in thy brother's eye, but considerest not the beam [wooden beam used in constructing houses] that is in thine own eye?" (Matt. 7:3; see Luke 6:41.)

They could just as well have been artificers or craftsmen of stone, which was much more available and used in the building trades. Note that the imagery in Jesus' teachings frequently includes the use of stone in building. (See, for example, Matt. 7:24–25; 16:18; Luke 14:28–30; 20:17–18.)

### "Sycamine" and "sycomore" trees (Luke 17:6; 19:4).

"If ye had faith as a grain of mustard seed, ye might say unto this sycamine tree, Be thou plucked up by the root, and be thou planted in the sea; and it should obey you." (Luke 17:6.) There is no other mention in the Bible of a sycamine tree, which is generally believed to be the black mulberry tree. In the parallel passages, Matthew and Mark both render "mountain" in place of "sycamine tree." The intent is the same: with faith even as minute as a mustard seed, miraculous results can be achieved.

The *sycomore* tree is not the same as the sycamine tree. While Jesus passed through Jericho, the chief tax collector for the Romans, who was a small man named Zacchaeus, wanted to see him: "He ran before, and climbed up into a sycomore tree to see him: for he was to pass that way." (Luke 19:4.)

The biblical sycomore tree (not the English/American tree called the sycamore) is known scientifically as *Ficus sycomorus* (thus the spelling in the New Tes-

98

tament) and is not found in the Near East above one thousand feet above sea level. In addition to his work as a sheep breeder, the prophet Amos was described as a cultivator or dresser of sycomores. (See Amos 7:14.) Since the sycomore does not grow near Tekoa, which is more than two thousand feet above sea level, Amos' work with sycomore figs must have taken him to the oases in the Jordan Valley or into the Shephelah (lowlands) of Judah.

*Ficus sycomorus* is a species of fig, or fig-mulberry, the fruit being like a fig and the leaf like the mulberry. The tree is known to grow to great size, sometimes attaining more than fifty feet in circumference, and is evergreen. Reproduction takes place only through the planting of cuttings, and the existence of the species (in Israel, at least) is totally dependent on cultivation. The fruit shoots forth on all parts of the stem, several figs on each leafless twig. The fruit is smaller than the regular fig and, though edible, is tasteless. In the land of Jesus, the sycomore tree grew in the mild coastal plains and in the Jordan Valley, where Jericho is situated and where Zacchaeus climbed one to see Jesus.

*"He would fain have filled his belly with the husks that the swine did eat." (Luke 15:16.)*

Yet another tree, the carob, or locust tree, is referred to in this line from the parable of the prodigal son. The Greek word *keratia,* which means "little horns" (apparently from the shape of the fruit), is variously translated "husks" or "pods." The carob tree, *ceratonia siliqua,* produces leathery brown pods containing beanlike

seeds used as a chocolate substitute in our own day. The seeds are remarkably consistent in weight and were used anciently to measure gem stones (the origin of our word *carat*).

Since the pods of the carob tree are supposed by some to be the locusts that John the Baptist ate (instead of insects), the pods are otherwise called St. John's Bread. High in sugar content, the pods of the carob were a staple fodder for cattle throughout eastern Mediterranean countries and were sometimes eaten by poorer people. The subhead scripture has the prodigal son wasting away to such a condition that he desired to eat what the swine were eating.

*"Much people . . . took branches of palm trees, and went forth to meet him." (John 12:12–13.)*

All of the Gospel writers recorded Jesus' triumphal entry into the city of Jerusalem at the beginning of the last week of his life, and all of them mention that people spread items of clothing and branches in front of him in his honor. John, however, is the only writer who specifies that the branches were from palm trees.

Palm trees do not generally grow on the slopes of the Mount of Olives, where the people had gathered to acclaim Jesus as their king. The natural habitat of the palm is a more moderate and tropical climate, though some were possibly growing in the Hinnom and other surrounding valleys. They could also have been transported up from Jericho for the Passover celebration, as is done to this day. The use

*Upper left:* Sycomore figs on the trunk and branches of a sycomore tree. *Upper right:* The carob, or locust, tree grows brown pods—the husks referred to in the parable of the prodigal son. (See Luke 15:16.) *Lower left:* A carob pod with beanlike seeds, used today as a chocolate substitute. *Lower right:* Palm branches were a symbol of Jewish independence.

of palm branches for Jesus' entry was not coincidental. Since the Hasmonaean period, palm branches had been a symbol of Jewish patriotism, independence, and triumph over enemies.

*"All flesh is as grass." (1 Pet. 1:24.)*

From a psalmist and from the prophet Isaiah, we learn the symbolism of grass, which persists through the end of both Testaments. "As for man, his days are as grass: as a flower of the field, so he flourisheth. For the wind passeth over it, and it is gone; and the place thereof shall know it no more." (Ps. 103:15–16.) "All flesh is grass, and all the goodliness thereof is as the flower of the field: the grass withereth, the flower fadeth: because the spirit of the Lord bloweth upon it: surely the people is grass. The grass withereth, the flower fadeth: but the word of our God shall stand forever." (Isa. 40:6–8.)

Grass was a physical similitude of the transitoriness of man. With the heavy rains of wintertime, grass flourishes and even spreads its velvety green carpet over the yeshimon (the barren wilderness); but with the wisp of the transitional khamsin, it is gone. The blades are vivacious and vigorous one day, vanished the next. So is the life of man.

But some things, like the word of God, are more timeless and permanent. "All flesh is as grass, and all the glory of man as the flower of grass. The grass withereth, and the flower thereof falleth away: but the word of the Lord endureth for ever. And this is the word which by the gospel is preached unto you." (1 Pet. 1:24–25.)

With such a transitory nature of temporal life on earth, it is comforting to know that there is also the permanence of an unchangeable and never-ending Providence: "If God so clothe the grass of the field, which to day is, and to morrow is cast into the oven, shall he not much more clothe you, O ye of little faith?" (Matt. 6:30.)

Prophets also called up natural comparisons in decrying the instability and transient character of riches and the ultimate emptiness of pursuing them: "The rich . . . is made low: because as the flower of the grass he shall pass away. For the sun is no sooner risen with a burning heat, but it withereth the grass, and the flower thereof falleth, and the grace of the fashion of it perisheth: so also shall the rich man fade away in his ways." (James 1:10–11.)

*"Do men gather grapes of thorns, or figs of thistles?" (Matt. 7:16); "of thorns men do not gather figs, nor of a bramble bush gather they grapes" (Luke 6:44).*

There grew in the land of Jesus a formidable abundance of thistles and thorns, and they could not escape the figurative eye of the prophets and Jesus. Thistles and thorns served only the role of affliction and distraction and annoyance. The parable of the four kinds of soil has seeds falling among thorns, which sprang up and choked the seeds. (See Matt. 13:7; Mark 4:7; Luke 8:7.) Those thorns represented cares and pleasures of this world and the deceitfulness of riches. (See Matt. 13:22; Mark 4:18–19; Luke 8:14.) Thorns seem never to symbolize anything good

101

Grass growing in the Judaean Wilderness in late winter or early spring.

Thistles and thorns symbolized affliction, distraction, and annoyance.

These may have been the kind of thorns woven together for Jesus' crown of thorns. (See Matt. 27:29.)

or positive. In short, "that which beareth thorns and briers is rejected, and is nigh unto cursing; whose end is to be burned." (Heb. 6:8.)

Paul had to endure "a thorn in the flesh" (2 Cor. 12:7), some weakness in his body or some trial in his life. While mocking Jesus, Roman soldiers wove thorns together in the shape of a crown and placed them on his head. (See Matt. 27:29; Mark 15:17; John 19:2.) Though only adding pain and insult to the already awful scene, yet in the eternal worldview of the early Christians, Jesus' crown of thorns was regarded as a necessary antecedent to his crown of glory. The thorn gave way to the Throne.

The thorns or thorn-branches constituting the "crown" placed on Jesus' head could have been woven together only if flexible. The traditional candidate is *Ziziphus spina-christi,* otherwise called the Christ-thorn. The etrog tree is also a producer of stout thorns that could have been used.

The bramble (*Rubus sanguineus*) is a prickly, evergreen vinelike shrub that produces an edible blackberry. It grows in all parts of the land, forming impenetrable thickets, especially along the riverbanks and by springs and swamps.

Again using nature as a comparison, Jesus' point was "every tree is known by his own fruit." (Luke 6:44.) Nobody gathers figs from thorns, and nobody gathers grapes from the bramble. Likewise, all people are known by their "fruits"—their words and their works, and their character and thoughts determine their actions.

*"A reed shaken with the wind . . . "*
*(Luke 7:24.)*

"Reed" is a general term for any tall, hard, hollow-stemmed grass or cane that grew along bodies of water in the Holy Land. Reeds mentioned in the New Testament were "shaken with the wind" (Matt. 11:7), were "bruised" (Matt. 12:20), were placed in Jesus' right hand as a mock scepter (see Matt. 27:29), were used to lift the vinegar-filled sponge to the lips of the crucified Lord (see Matt. 27:48), and were used as a measuring rod (see Rev. 11:1; 21:15–16).

The first usage was part of a question Jesus posed to followers of John the Baptist, "What went ye out into the wilderness to see? A reed shaken with the wind?" In other words, Jesus had asked, "Why did you go out into the Judaean desert? To see the common reeds blowing in the wind?" No, they had gone to see a prophet, and one of the greatest prophets. (See Matt. 11:11.)

The second usage, "a bruised reed shall he not break," refers to the gentleness of the Messiah. Here the reed is a type of humanity, and the Messiah, who finds many reeds bruised by the storms of life, is inclined to bind up and heal, rather than to break and destroy.

*"They gave him vinegar to drink mingled with gall." (Matt. 27:34.)*

On the cross Jesus thirsted, and, according to Matthew's report, soldiers offered him cheap wine mixed with gall (Hebrew, *rosh;* Greek, *choles*). Gall is some substance that is bitter, even poisonous. Some believe it to be the juice of the opium poppy, which causes heavy sleep and insensibility (the *rosh,* or "head," possibly even alluding to the poppy head).

It was used in the Old Testament for a parallel with wormwood (*Artemisia absinthium*), a repulsive plant always used metaphorically for something that is bitter or cruel. The Old Testament's contexts of *rosh,* however, seem always to be poisonous. (See, for example, Deut. 29:18; Amos 6:12; Lam. 3:15, 19.) Its poisonous nature gave rise to the idiomatic expression, "the gall of bitterness." (Acts 8:23.) The gall in the vinegar offered to Jesus was presumably to act as a painkiller.

*"Consider the lilies how they grow."*
*(Luke 12:27.)*

Lilies are flowers that grow from a bulb, like the iris, crocus, hyacinth, tulip, and narcissus. Though not a true lily, the common crown anemone, *Anemone coronaria,* is the likely object of Jesus' superlative comparison to Solomon. By saying that the once-wise king in all his glory was not arrayed like one of the lilies, we are to understand that the flush of colorful spring anemones scattered over all the hills, valleys, and plains would produce in the eyes of the beholder genuine admiration and awe for the elegant beauty of one of God's simple creations. If God cares for the smallest works of his hands, surely he will care for and provide for humankind, his crowning creation.

NOTE

1. Mishnah, *Pirke Aboth, the Sayings of the Fathers,* 22.

104

# LIVESTOCK, HERDING, AND FISHING

*"I am the good shepherd." (John 10:11.)*

Shepherding stands with farming as the two great biblical occupations. Sheep have been inextricably tied to the pastoral economy and theology of the people of Israel since their beginning. In the biblical books of law and history, sheep are frequently mentioned in connection with their vital domestic role in the household and community ecosystem and in sacrificial practices. Sheep were vital to the Roman-period Jews because of the products derived from them: meat, wool, skins (see Heb. 11:37), and milk (see 1 Cor. 9:7).

In the New Testament, there is an occasional statement about actual sheep. At Jesus' birth, there were "shepherds abiding in the field, keeping watch over their flock by night" (Luke 2:8); and at the beginning of his ministry, Jesus "found in the temple those that sold oxen and sheep and doves, and the changers of money sitting: and when he had made a scourge of small cords, he drove them all out of the temple, and the sheep" (John 2:14–15). The report of one of his great miracles opens with a geographical note: "Now there is at Jerusalem by the sheep market

a pool." (John 5:2; see "Go, wash in the pool of Siloam" in chapter 12.)

In the wisdom literature and the prophetic books, however, sheep are used more as a symbol of the Israelites themselves: "We thy people and sheep of thy pasture will give thee thanks for ever." (Ps. 79:13.) "He is our God; and we are the people of his pasture, and the sheep of his hand." (Ps. 95:7.) "All we like sheep have gone astray." (Isa. 53:6.) "My people hath been lost sheep: their shepherds have caused them to go astray. . . . Israel is a scattered sheep; the lions have driven him away: first the king of Assyria hath devoured him; and last this . . . king of Babylon hath broken his bones." (Jer. 50:6, 17.)

In the literature, then, the uses of sheep, the sheepfold, and the shepherd were as symbols. Earth life was seen as a desert, the children of God as scattered sheep wandering hungry and helpless, needing guidance from the Good Shepherd who desires to lead them over the trails and trials of life, to bring them all back into the safety of the fold. "When he saw the multitudes, he was moved with compassion on them, because they

*Top left:* Besides being a mainstay of Israelite economy, sheep were used in the Bible as a symbol of the Israelites themselves. *Top right to bottom left:* The process of shearing sheep and hanging the wool to dry. *Bottom right:* A sheepfold in the Judaean Desert.

fainted, and were scattered abroad, as sheep having no shepherd." (Matt. 9:36.)

Two of the noble and esteemed positions in Israel were the shepherd and the king. David was the role model, having shepherded his family's flocks and then shepherded his nation as king. David knew that there was a Shepherd greater than he. He had watched over and cared for his family's sheep, but he exulted in proclaiming, "The Lord is *my* shepherd." (Ps. 23:1; italics added.)

Jesus was seen as "the son of David" (Matt. 1:1), serving the same revered roles. He was first "the great shepherd of the sheep" (Heb. 13:20), "the chief Shepherd" (1 Pet. 5:4), and then the King, whose "kingdom is not of this world" (John 18:36). "For ye were as sheep going astray; but are now returned unto the Shepherd . . . of your souls." (1 Pet. 2:25.)

One of the longest, most sustained and poignant metaphors in the Bible, another of the classic and timeless illustrations of comparing something in nature to the human experience, is the detailed exposition of Jesus about his people as sheep and himself as Shepherd. In it we find much instructive detail about the work of the shepherd and characteristics of the sheep.

"I say unto you, He that entereth not by the door into the sheepfold, but climbeth up some other way, the same is a thief and a robber. But he that entereth in by the door is the shepherd of the sheep. To him the porter [doorkeeper] openeth; and the sheep hear his voice: and he calleth his own sheep by name, and leadeth them out. And when he putteth forth his own sheep, he goeth before them, and the sheep follow him: for they know his voice. And a stranger will they not follow, but will flee from him: for they know not the voice of strangers. . . .

"Verily, verily, I say unto you, I am the door of the sheep. . . . By me if any man enter in, he shall be saved, and shall go in and out, and find pasture. The thief cometh not, but for to steal, and to kill, and to destroy: I am come that they might have life, and that they might have it more abundantly.

"I am the good shepherd: the good shepherd giveth his life for the sheep. But he that is an hireling, and not the shepherd, whose own the sheep are not, seeth the wolf coming, and leaveth the sheep, and fleeth: and the wolf catcheth them, and scattereth the sheep. The hireling fleeth, because he is an hireling, and careth not for the sheep. I am the good shepherd, and know my sheep, and am known of mine. As the Father knoweth me, even so know I the Father: and I lay down my life for the sheep." (John 10:1–15.)

Jesus saw his faithful followers as a "little flock" (Luke 12:32) that needed to be fed and protected from the perils of their earthly pasture. If a sheep were to stray and be in danger, it was incumbent on the true shepherd, loving the sheep as much as his own life, to leave the secure ones and go out to rescue the one. "What man of you, having an hundred sheep, if he lose one of them, doth not leave the ninety and nine . . . and go after that which is lost, until he find it? And when he hath found it, he layeth it on his shoulders, rejoicing. . . . I say unto you, that likewise joy shall be in heaven over one sinner that repenteth, more than over ninety and nine just persons, which need no repentance." (Luke 15:3–7.)

Jesus had previously asked, "What man shall there be among you, that shall have one sheep, and if it fall into a pit . . . will he not lay hold on it, and lift it out?" The follow-up question profoundly points the genuine disciple in the direction of his life's work, "How much then is a man better than a sheep?" (Matt. 12:11–12.)

The Lord knew that his flock would lose their Shepherd, "for it is written, I will smite the shepherd, and the sheep of the flock shall be scattered abroad." (Matt. 26:31; see Zech. 13:7.) He prepared them for that loss. He emphasized to Peter three times, "Feed my lambs," "Feed my sheep." (John 21:15–16.) Peter himself later wrote to local shepherd-leaders, "Feed the flock of God which is among you, taking the oversight thereof, not by constraint, but willingly; . . . neither as being lords over God's heritage, but being ensamples to the flock." (1 Pet. 5:2–3.) Paul likewise told others, "Take heed therefore unto yourselves, and to all the flock . . . to feed the church of God." (Acts 20:28.)

*"Behold the Lamb of God." (John 1:29.)*

The Good Shepherd and his disciple-shepherds knew that in the ensuing generations some of the sheep would find themselves in peril and even be sacrificed for the cause of God, "as it is written, For thy sake we are killed all the day long; we are accounted as sheep for the slaughter." (Rom. 8:36; see Ps. 44:22.) Some of those who were sacrificed must have hoped to follow their Lord's example, as it was written, "He was led as a sheep to the slaughter; and like a lamb dumb before his shearer, so opened he not his mouth." (Acts 8:32; see Isa. 53:7.) A lamb or sheep is one of the few animals that does not make a protest at its time of slaughter but actually remains hushed, pacific, and submissive to the end.

John the Baptist saw that analogy too. Twice in John 1, the prophet announced, referring to Jesus, "Behold the Lamb of God." (Vv. 29, 36.) Not only were the people of Israel referred to as sheep, but Jesus himself was also deemed a young and tender sheep, or a lamb. Paul called him "our passover" who was "sacrificed for us," referring to the sacrificial lamb at Passover. (See 1 Cor. 5:7.)

Of all New Testament writers, only John called Jesus the Lamb of God, twice quoting John the Baptist, and twenty-eight times mentioning the Lamb in the book of Revelation. There the Lamb is personified. He was slain (see 5:12), his blood was able to cleanse (see 7:14), and he was worshiped (see 5:8.) The Lamb felt wrath (see 6:16) and fought a war (see 17:14.) He had a marriage supper (see 19:9) and was married to his bride (see 19:7; 21:9). He possessed a book of life (see 13:8; 21:27) and a song (see 15:3) and served as light for the city of God (see 21:23).

*"A shepherd divideth his sheep from the goats." (Matt. 25:32.)*

Shepherds herded sheep and goats, and both were valued for food and clothing. Goats provided food in the form of meat—the prodigal son's brother, for instance, complained that his father had never given him a kid to make merry with his friends (see Luke 15:29)—and milk. One goat could yield several pints a day, which were used to make leben (a type of yogurt) and cheese. Goatskins were made into bottles for making butter, and the hair was useful in making tents (the ancient Tabernacle—see Ex. 25:3–8; 26:7–13—and family tents).

The goat was selected in early Israelite history as the "scapegoat." On the Day of Atonement, the high priest laid his hands on the goat's head and symbolically placed on the goat all the sins of the people. The scapegoat was then chased into the wilderness, which figuratively expulsed the nation's sins—"the goat shall bear upon him all their iniquities unto a land not inhabited." (Lev. 16:20–23.) The blood of goats was shed for centuries to ritually cleanse and sanctify the people. (See Heb. 9.) In his elaborate exposition on the purpose of all those sacrifices, however, Paul remonstrated that, "it is not possible that the blood of bulls and of goats should take away sins." (Heb. 10:4.)

All those sacrificial offerings made on the great altar of the Temple were but a type, a foreshadowing of the sacrifice of the Lamb of God. We note that a *Lamb* was what would be slain for the sins of the world. There seems to have been, even in antiquity, a symbolic dichotomy between sheep and goats. Sheep were light in color, goats dark. The people of God were often identified as the sheep of his fold, but never as goats. Heightening the contrast,

Jesus proclaimed that, in the day of judgment, "before him shall be gathered all nations: and he shall separate them one from another, as a shepherd divideth his sheep from the goats: and he shall set the sheep on his right hand, but the goats on the left." (Matt. 25:32–33.)

Though both sheep and goats were essential in the pastoral economy of Israel, yet for the purpose of illustrating a doctrinal point, the two animals were called on to represent opposites, those worthy and those unworthy to enter God's kingdom. Those who are full of light, not in skin color but in their spirit, will be set on the right hand, the place of honor and blessing, while those who are dark in spirit will be set on the left, the place of condemnation and punishment.

*"Take nothing for your journey, neither staves, nor scrip."*
*(Luke 9:3.)*

The shepherd's equipment is mentioned in connection with supplies normally taken on journeys, but which the Lord commanded not to be taken on missions. The staff was a long stick used for a variety of purposes: maneuvering through the rocky hill country, controlling movement of the sheep, and even using as a weapon if necessary. The scrip was a small leather bag used to carry food and other provisions. It was often distinguished from the purse, which carried money. Disciples were discouraged from taking staff, scrip, shoes, bread, money, or two coats. (See Matt. 10:9–10; Luke 9:3; 10:4.) Instead of providing for all their own

*Top left:* Goats are hardy and valuable to the economy. The lips and mouth of the goat are so tough, it can eat the prickliest thorns without damage or pain. *Top right:* Cleaning goats' hair for making tents. *Center left:* Dark-haired goats and light-haired sheep are frequently found together in herds. *Center right:* Twice in the Gospels, Jesus used camels in hyperboles: a camel going through a needle's eye (see Matt. 19:24), and swallowing a camel (see Matt. 23:24). *Bottom left:* The lowly but useful and respected ass. *Bottom right:* To the Jews, pigs were the embodiment of impurity and ill repute.

needs, they were to trust in God for vital provisions.

### "A servant plowing or feeding cattle . . . " (Luke 17:7.)

In one of his many stories, Jesus spoke of servants out in the fields "plowing or feeding cattle." In this phrase, we have reference once again to the two main occupations of ancient Israel: agriculture and herding/shepherding. The "cattle" spoken of in this passage are "small cattle," that is, sheep and goats. The Greek verb *poimaino* means to herd, tend, or lead sheep and goats to pasture.

The other of the two occurrences of *cattle* in the New Testament is the reference to Jacob and his children and his "cattle" drinking from Jacob's Well. (See John 4:12.) Again, cattle (Greek, *thremma*) are domesticated animals, particularly sheep and goats.

### "I have bought five yoke of oxen, and I go to prove them." (Luke 14:19.)

Besides sheep and goats, other livestock are noted in the New Testament: chickens (cocks and hens), camels, asses, swine, and oxen. Few animals in the ancient rural economy of the Israelites were more highly esteemed and put to use than the cow or ox. The operations of farming were quite dependent on them: oxen were used for plowing (see Luke 14:19; 17:7), threshing (see 1 Cor. 9:9; 1 Tim. 5:18), drawing wagons, and carrying supplies. They were eaten as food (see Matt. 22:4; Luke 15:23–30) and slaughtered for sacrifices (see John 2:14–15). Cows also supplied milk and butter.

When two animals plowed together, a yoke was used, which consisted of a wooden beam laid across the top of the animals' necks and fastened together with leather or rope straps under the necks. The Mosaic law prohibited yoking two different beasts together, such as an ox and an ass. The unequal pull could cause the weaker or smaller of the animals discomfort and pain. Rather than being prejudicial or exclusivist, Paul's counsel, "Be ye not unequally yoked together with unbelievers" (2 Cor. 6:14), was meant to protect the partners from experiencing the unequal marital pull that could cause serious discomfort and pain to one or the other or both.

In some cases, a yoke could be a negative, undesirable thing, as the yoke the Judaizers would place on members of the Christian Church, insisting still on circumcision, the token of conformity and strict adherence to the old Mosaic law: "Why tempt ye God, to put a yoke upon the neck of the disciples, which neither our fathers nor we were able to bear?" (Acts 15:10.) Paul wrote, "Stand fast therefore in the liberty wherewith Christ hath made us free, and be not entangled again with the yoke of bondage." (Gal. 5:1.)

On the other hand, a yoke could be a positive, desirable thing, as the yoke of submission and obedience and its consequent freedom from the weight of sin: "Take my yoke upon you, and learn of me; for I am meek and lowly in heart: and ye shall find rest unto your souls. For my yoke is easy, and my burden is light." (Matt. 11:29–30.) Just as the yoke kept oxen steadily pulling together in a com-

111

mon direction, so the yoke of Christ helps members of his kingdom to work together in the common cause; and the burden it requires a member to carry is light compared to the burden of those who labor under the heavy weight of disobedience and sin.

### "As a hen gathereth her chickens under her wings . . . " (Matt. 23:37.)

The same Messiah who would not strive or cry or break a bruised reed or quench a smoking flax (see Matt. 12:19–20, quoting Isaiah) tenderly but fiercely lamented the Holy City and the obstinance and recalcitrance of its citizens: "O Jerusalem, Jerusalem, thou that killest the prophets, and stonest them which are sent unto thee, how often would I have gathered thy children together, even as a hen gathereth her chickens under her wings, and ye would not!" (Matt. 23:37).

The hen is one of the edible fowls mentioned in the Bible. The Greek word *ornis* actually means bird or fowl, not only a hen. God assumed the image of a bird hovering over Jerusalem, the place that he had chosen to make his dwelling place on earth. It was a familiar image. "As birds [hovering over their young], so will the Lord of hosts defend Jerusalem; defending also he will deliver it; and passing over he will preserve it." (Isa. 31:5.)

As with most species, the bird watches over and is highly protective of its young. The Lord had said that, if his people were obedient, he would be their guard and protector; he would fight their battles; he would hold them close and keep them safe. The psalmists sang that same refrain,

"Hide me under the shadow of thy wings, from the wicked that oppress me, from my deadly enemies, who compass me about." (Ps. 17:8–9.) "My soul trusteth in thee: yea, in the shadow of thy wings will I make my refuge, until these calamities be overpast." (Ps. 57:1.)

God had regularly sent his servants to warn the people how to remain long upon the land that the Lord their God had given them and to advise them of the requirements of security. "The Lord God of their fathers sent to them by his messengers, rising up betimes, and sending; because he had compassion on his people, and on his dwelling place: but they mocked the messengers of God, and despised his words, and misused his prophets, until the wrath of the Lord arose against his people, till there was no remedy." (2 Chron. 36:15–16.)

So it was again. Jesus lamented that the Holy City was not the city of holiness. Jerusalemites had killed the prophets and were about to kill him. The deepest pathos surrounds Jesus' sigh of desire to gather his brood protectively under his wing. The same God who had sat under the wings of the cherubim could "arise with healing in his wings" (Mal. 4:2) and could keep his people out from under the wings of the Roman eagle, but—"ye would not!"

The only mention of the male, the rooster, is in connection with Peter's denial of his acquaintance with Jesus. "Verily I say unto thee," Jesus told Peter, "That this night, before the cock crow, thou shalt deny me thrice." (Matt. 26:34.) Matthew recorded that when Peter was identified as a disciple, "then began he to curse and to swear, saying, I know not the man. And immediately the cock crew. And Peter remembered the word of Jesus, which said unto him, Before the cock crow, thou shalt deny me thrice. And he went out, and wept bitterly." (Matt. 26:74–75.)

The time of cockcrow by Roman reckoning was during the third watch of the night, between midnight and three A.M. During the terrifying darkness of that tragic night, before the earliest call of morning, Peter the Rock would be crushed bitterly by the suffering of Jesus that he could not help relieve.

## "It is easier for a camel to go through the eye of a needle." (Matt. 19:24.)

The camel is mentioned in only three contexts in the New Testament. The first is John the Baptist being clothed with camel's hair and a leather (animal-skin) girdle. (See Matt. 3:4; Mark 1:6.) The second is the analogy Jesus made between a camel going through the eye of a needle and a rich man entering the kingdom of God. (See Matt. 19:24; Mark 10:25; Luke 18:25.)

The camel going through the eye of a needle does not refer to some hypothetical little gate in or alongside a main city gate, through which a camel is supposed to edge his way on its knees after being stripped of its burden. The present writer has seen the remnants of numerous ancient cities and gates throughout the Near East, and his conclusion is that such a little gate did not exist! Such a notion is a figment of the imagination of someone who was probably trying to explain the image without understanding an important figure of speech that Jesus used.

The Greek word used for "needle," *raphis,* means "a sewing needle." In the Hebrew text of this passage, *hamakhat* is used, which is also the ordinary word for a sewing needle. To make his point, Jesus was using a purposefully extreme exaggeration, a literary device common to Hebrew tradition called *hyperbole.*

The third use of *camel* is in another hyperbole Jesus gave concerning scribes and Pharisees: "Ye blind guides, which strain at a gnat, and swallow a camel." (Matt. 23:24.) The Prophet Joseph Smith explained this hyperbole of extremes by comparing it to extremes in conduct. He added this phrase to the verse: "who make yourselves appear unto men that ye would not commit the least sin, and yet ye yourselves, trangress the whole law." (JST, Matt. 23:21.)

Following are other examples of hyperbole, marked by italics:

Deuteronomy 1:28 (of the Israelites' fear of the Amorites): "The people is greater and taller than we; the cities are great and *walled up to heaven.*"

Judges 20:16 (of the combat expertise of warriors of Benjamin): "Every one could sling stones *at an hair breadth, and not miss*" (the word "breadth" does not appear in the original; the Hebrew text says they could sling stones *at a hair* and not miss!).

2 Samuel 1:23 (in David's lament over the deaths of Saul and Jonathan): "They were *swifter than eagles,* they were *stronger than lions.*"

Lamentations 2:11 (the depth of grief and

113

sorrow at the loss of the Holy City): "Mine eyes do fail with tears, my bowels are troubled, *my liver is poured upon the earth.*"

Lamentations 3:48: "*Mine eye runneth down with rivers of water* for the destruction . . . of my people."

Matthew 5:29: "If thy right eye offend thee, *pluck it out, and cast it from thee:* for it is profitable for thee that one of thy members should perish, and not that thy whole body should be cast into hell."

John 12:19 (perplexity of the Pharisees after the raising of Lazarus): "Perceive ye how ye prevail nothing? behold, *the world is gone after him.*"

John 21:25: "There are also many other things which Jesus did, the which, if they should be written every one, I suppose that *even the world itself could not contain the books* that should be written."

Jesus did not really mean, of course, if your right eye is offensive in some way, to dig into the socket and pluck it out! The use of hyperbole makes the spiritual message more impressive and vividly engraves the meaning on the memory of the spiritually receptive: if there is some fault of character or sin destructive to the soul, get rid of that fault lest it destroy the whole soul.

To make his point, Jesus exaggerated the sums of money involved in the parable of the unforgiving servant. (See Matt. 18: 23–35.) Ten thousand talents, which the

servant owed the king, was an enormous sum — millions of dollars. The hundred pence which the fellow-servant owed his friend was a small debt. The striking contrast makes the lesson of the parable more impressive.

In similar fashion, Jesus, in his scathing rebukes of the hypocritical religious leaders and the rich, used strong metaphors: *swallowing a camel* and *going through the eye of a needle!* When he illustrated the difficulty for rich men to earn the blessing of celestial glory, Jesus adopted a common literary device of his time to stress the hazards and challenges of having great riches. Knowing how wealth and prosperity generally work on the human personality, Jesus could appropriately and perceptively say, "It is easier for a camel to go through the eye of a needle, than for a rich man to enter into the kingdom of God."

*"Thy King cometh unto thee, meek, and sitting upon an ass." (Matt. 21:5.)*

The ass was a useful and respected animal in the ancient Near East. The number of asses a man possessed was a measure of his wealth. Asses were associated with royalty, even with the Messiah. Zechariah had heralded the glad tidings of the messianic era with the following prophecy: "Rejoice greatly, O daughter of Zion; shout, O daughter of Jerusalem: behold, thy King cometh unto thee: he is just, and having salvation; lowly, and riding upon an ass, and upon a colt the foal of an ass." (Zech. 9:9.)

We learn from the prophet that the royal entry into Jerusalem on an ass was a symbol of humility, in token of peace. Riding a horse would have symbolized war and fighting strength, but the Messiah was coming, not to conquer, but to save. It might have made the Romans smile to see this acclaimed Deliverer approaching on an ass, and it might have confused and angered the Jews who anticipated an armed confrontation and overthrow of the Romans. But the triumphal entry was no meaningless pageantry or seditious demonstration; it was an open acknowledgment by Jesus as the Prince of Peace of his kingly and messianic titles.

Mark, Luke, and John mention a colt only, whereas the text of Matthew clearly indicates that the disciples brought an ass and a colt (the colt being the male foal, or offspring, of an ass). Matthew, or a later editor, seems to have sought meticulous fulfillment of the prophecy of Zechariah by specifying two animals, although Zechariah's prophetic preview of the Messiah is couched in the poetic structure called parallelism, which presents an image or subject in two parallel phrases. There was actually only one animal intended — Jesus, of course, could ride only one animal. The discrepancy in the number of animals is resolved by a simple correction that the Prophet Joseph Smith made: Matthew 21:2 and 5 in the Joseph Smith Translation indicate that only one animal was involved.

*" . . . nigh unto the mountains a great herd of swine feeding." (Mark 5:11.)*

Swine, or pigs, are involved in two episodes in the New Testament, one actual and one literary. The Synoptic Gos-

pels (Matthew, Mark, and Luke) all record a miracle of Jesus casting evil spirits out of a man to the east of the Sea of Galilee (see "Gergesa and Gadara" in chapter 2), whereupon the evil spirits entered the bodies of swine grazing nearby and caused them to rush violently into the lake and be drowned (see Matt. 8:30–32).

The other episode involving swine was in Jesus' story of the prodigal son who went into a far (gentile) country and, after wasting his substance with riotous living, found himself working during a famine by feeding swine, desiring to eat even the carob pods that the swine ate. (See Luke 15:13–16.) From that story, we understand that Jews considered any connection with swine to be the lowest, most despicable condition to which one could fall.

Another evidence that swine represented what was depraved and disreputable was the proverb Jesus created, again in parallelistic form: "Give not that which is holy unto the dogs, neither cast ye your pearls before swine." (Matt. 7:6.)

*"I will make you fishers of men."* *(Matt. 4:19.)*

Shipping was a convenient method of transportation on the Sea of Galilee in New Testament times. In Matthew, we have considerable detail about Jesus' travels by boat on the lake: "When he was entered into a ship, his disciples followed him." (8:23.) "He entered into a ship, and passed over, and came into his own city [Capernaum]." (9:1.) "He departed thence by ship into a desert place apart [Bethsaida]." (14:13.) "He sent away the multitude, and took ship, and came into the coasts of Magdala." (15:39.)

And on another occasion, the Lord used a boat for teaching: "Great multitudes were gathered together unto him, so that he went into a ship, and sat; and the whole multitude stood on the shore. And he spake many things unto them." (Matt. 13:2–3.)

Galilaeans, having a lake in their region that was full of fish, engaged in fishing as an occupation. There are very few references to fish and fishing later in the New Testament, but the Gospel writers constantly noted the work of the fishermen, particularly of the apostles at the Sea of Galilee. Fishing was a prosperous industry. Taricheae, the Greek name of Magdala, means "fish salting," relating to the active commercial fishing occurring there. The apostles who left behind their ships and nets were decidedly breaking from a lucrative vocation.

Fish were involved in several miracles that Jesus performed. For example, with a few fish, he fed a group of over five thousand and a group of over four thousand. (See Matt. 14:15–21; 15:32–38.) More than once Jesus instructed his fishermen-disciples to cast their nets into a different spot from where they were fishing, and they were provided an overabundance of fish, "and their net brake." (Luke 5:6.) Commercial fishing was and still is done at night. The fish school nearer the surface of the lake at night and remain deeper during the warmth of the day—making the miraculous catches of fish during the day all the more unusual. (See Luke 5:5–6; John 21:3–6.)

On yet another occasion, in order to provide for the tribute money, Jesus told Peter to go fishing just off shore, "Take up the fish that first cometh up; and when thou hast opened his mouth, thou shalt find a piece of money: that take, and give unto them for me and thee." (Matt. 17:27.) Some have wondered if this particular fish was what today is called "St. Peter's fish." The St. Peter's fish (*Tilapia galilaea*) is a mouth-breeder and has been known to carry pebbles, bottle caps, and other foreign objects in its mouth. Perhaps the supernatural conditions that came together to produce such an extraordinary incident are not so inexplicable after all, though the knowledge of the exact location of a fish *with a coin in its mouth* is still most miraculous!

Some of the fisherman's equipment is identified in the New Testament. Recognizing the resurrected Jesus walking along the edge of the lake, Peter, who was half naked, put on his "fisher's coat" and dove into the water to swim to shore. (See John 21:7.) Fishing was done by angling—casting in a hook (see Matt. 17:27)—or by using two kinds of nets.

The cast net was usually thrown from shore, its weighted edges sinking to the bottom and trapping any fish, and then hauled in. Simon Peter and Andrew his brother were casting a net into the sea when Jesus called to them to follow him. (See Matt. 4:18.) The drag net (otherwise called the *seine*—pronounced *sane*) was much longer and was spread out over a large area and then dragged in by the boats. (See Luke 5:4; John 21:6.)

As with most other human occupations, fishing would not escape the eye of the poet and the prophet, and especially not the eye of the master teacher: "The kingdom of heaven is like unto a net, that was cast into the sea, and gathered of every kind: which, when it was full, they drew to shore, and sat down, and gathered the good into vessels, but cast the bad away. So shall it be at the end of the world: the angels shall come forth, and sever the wicked from among the just." (Matt. 13:47–49.)

# ANIMAL LIFE

*"He was there in the wilderness . . . with the wild beasts." (Mark 1:13.)*

Besides sheep and goats, oxen, camels, asses, swine, and fish, the New Testament speaks of other members of the world of fauna, some few domesticated, most wild. Peter's vision of beasts coming down out of heaven differentiates between "fourfooted beasts of the earth [those common to Israelite economy], and wild beasts, and creeping things, and fowls of the air." (See Acts 10:12; 11:6.)

Mark 1:13 in its entirety has Jesus in the wilderness for forty days, sometime tempted by Satan, and accompanied by wild beasts and angels. Those animals that lived in the wild we will divide into birds, snakes, insects, and mammals (other than those discussed in the previous chapter).

*"Behold the fowls of the air." (Matt. 6:26.)*

Since the land of Israel is on one of the world's major bird migration routes, with over 350 species of birds represented in the land, it would be surprising if Bible writers had not mentioned birds and included them in their imagery. The Bible specifically names thirty-five species. All nocturnals known today are spoken of in Holy Writ, also all of the owl family. Storks, doves, quail, and vultures are particularly well known in the land of the Bible.

Jesus made various observations regarding the habits of birds: "Behold the fowls of the air: for they sow not, neither do they reap, nor gather into barns; yet your heavenly Father feedeth them. Are ye not much better than they?" (Matt. 6:26.) "The birds of the air have nests; but the Son of man hath not where to lay his head." (Matt. 8:20.) "Some seeds fell by the way side, and the fowls came and devoured them up." (Matt. 13:4.) The mustard seed "is the least of all seeds: but when it is grown, it . . . becometh a tree, so that the birds of the air come and lodge in the branches thereof." (Matt. 13:32.)

*"Be ye therefore . . . harmless as doves." (Matt. 10:16.)*

Since early history, doves have symbolized peace, purity, and innocence. Noah released a dove several times from the ark to ascertain whether the flood waters had subsided. (See Genesis 8.) The return of the dove with an olive branch in its beak has long since been associated with overtures toward peace. The Lord used Jonah (Hebrew, *Yonah,* meaning "dove") to extend an offer of peace and forgiveness to the Ninevites rather than the prophesied destruction.

For centuries, the pure white dove was offered up as a sacrifice on the great altar of the Temple. For those who were too poor to afford a lamb for the ritual of purification after childbirth, two doves or young pigeons were allowed. (See Lev. 12:8.) After her forty-day period of purification in isolation, Mary, with husband Joseph and baby Jesus, journeyed to the Temple: "When the days of her purification according to the law of Moses were accomplished, they brought [Jesus] to Jerusalem, to present him to the Lord . . . and to offer a sacrifice according to that which is said in the law of the Lord, A pair of turtledoves, or two young pigeons." (Luke 2:22, 24.)

Doves were sold in the Temple porticoes for the above purpose. The law itself was holy, and the execution of the law was right, but motives were still crucial: "Jesus went up to Jerusalem, and found in the temple those that sold oxen and sheep and doves, and the changers of money sitting: and when he had made a scourge of small cords, he drove them all out of the temple, and the sheep, and the oxen; and poured out the changers' money, and overthrew the tables; and said unto them that sold doves, Take these things hence; make not my Father's house an house of merchandise." (John 2:13–16.)

Jesus left no doubt as to who he was. The Temple was his Father's house, and he did not want to see it desecrated by greedy merchandisers who seldom entertained a worthy thought about the sacredness of their sales. Annas and Caiaphas, who would become two of the chief persecutors of the Lord, could have been among the most furious over this daring act of Jesus, as they were undoubtedly prominent shareholders in the sacrificial animal businesses.

At the beginning of Jesus' ministry, we find Jesus at the lowest place on earth, standing in the Jordan River, being baptized by John. As he came up out of the water, "the heavens were opened unto him, and he saw the Spirit of God descending like a dove." (Matt. 3:16.) Or, as Luke recorded, "the Holy Ghost descended in a bodily shape like a dove upon him" (Luke 3:22) — that is, the Holy Ghost, having bodily shape, descended as a dove descends, and rested upon Jesus, "and John bare record, saying, I saw the Spirit descending from heaven like a dove, and it abode upon him" (John 1:32).

According to the Prophet Joseph Smith, the dove is the sign of the Holy Ghost's presence,[1] so an actual dove was likely present. Those disciples who would travel and teach and testify must have the Holy Ghost with them, and as they were "sheep in the midst of wolves," they would have to be "wise as serpents, and harmless as doves." (Matt. 10:16.)

*"Consider the ravens." (Luke 12:24.)*

Illustrating the providence of God, Jesus taught his disciples, "Take no thought for your life, what ye shall eat; neither for the body, what he shall put on. . . .

120

Consider the ravens: for they neither sow nor reap; which neither have storehouse nor barn; and God feedeth them: how much more are ye better than the fowls?" (Luke 12:22, 24.)

This was Jesus' hyperbolic way of encouraging his disciples to divest themselves of constant preoccupation or anxiety with worldly survival. He did not intend for people to abandon their mortal labors and wait for God to provide. Notice, he said, the ravens (crows, or birds in general, as in the other accounts); they do not plant and cultivate and harvest the fields; they do not store up great quantities of supplies in barns; but God takes care of them.

The lesson is one of faith and trust. We do what we can, and then we have confidence that God will take care of us. God wants his children to be submissive and dependent, to look to him and live. We labor; God provides.

The ravens were of little consequence, but God nevertheless cared for them. So also the sparrows: "Not one of them is forgotten before God." (Luke 12:6.) If God watches over his minor creations, then what of his crowning creation, his own children? "Fear not therefore: ye are of more value than many sparrows." (Luke 12:7.)

*"O generation of vipers . . . "*
*(Matt. 3:7.)*

Three times in Matthew, we have John and Jesus referring to their religious antagonists as vipers. (See 3:7; 12:34; 23:33.) The Palestine viper (*Vipera palaestina*) is the most dangerous and poisonous of all snakes in the land of Israel. Though frightening, the tongue of the viper is harmless. It serves as a smell-taste organ that darts in and out of the mouth, gathering air particles that are deciphered inside the brain. The front fangs are the potent weapon; they are sunk into a victim, and poison is secreted from glands to the wound. The venom destroys red corpuscles, causing hemorrhage, which, if not immediately and properly cared for, can result in death.

The author had a thirty-eight-year-old male student, large and sturdy, working in the banana fields of a kibbutz near the Sea of Galilee. One day he tried to save a snake from the hands of other students who uncovered it and intended to kill it. When he picked it up with his fingers to remove it from danger, the viper somehow elongated itself and swung around and sank its fangs into his forefinger.

Immediately after the bite, kibbutz personnel rushed him to a nearby hospital where he remained for three days of observation. They released him, but after spending a few hours at our school in Jerusalem, the pain in his finger was still so intense that we rushed him in the middle of the night to the emergency room of a Jerusalem hospital. The student remained in the hospital for twelve more days. Doctors tried every kind of painkiller to ease his periodic agony. Now and then his whole body writhed with pain from his finger. The finger increased to double its normal size, and the tissues inside turned a deep black color. We feared that they might have to amputate his finger, maybe even his hand.

The student was released from the Je-

121

rusalem hospital to fly back to the U.S.A. with his student group, and there he was admitted to another medical center. Several months passed before he recovered completely from those venomous fangs that had sunk just a fraction of an inch into his finger. Had the poison been injected into a smaller, more fragile body, we might have lost a student.

That was the only encounter we have had in many years of students and thousands of hours in banana fields and throughout the varied terrain of the Holy Land. We learned some vivid lessons about the viper from just that one incident, and we understand why John and Jesus used the viper in their figurative denunciation of those whom they considered hypocrites.

The Palestine viper bites only when it is trodden on. Some Sadducees, Pharisees, scribes, and lawyers apparently felt that they were being trodden on. And there was venom in their mouths. While they were lashing out, intending to strike some death blows to their would-be victims, John and Jesus issued some defensive warnings to beware of their poison.

*"I give unto you power to tread on serpents and scorpions." (Luke 10:19.)*

The word *snake* does not appear in the King James Bible; instead, the word *serpent* is used. As would be expected, the serpent is used both literally and figuratively in the scriptures, more often the latter in the New Testament. "Ye serpents, ye generation of vipers," Jesus labeled certain hypocrites. (Matt. 23:33.) James taught that

men have tamed every kind of beast and serpent, "but the tongue can no man tame; it is an unruly evil, full of deadly poison." (James 3:8.) To the serpent was attributed the characteristic of cunning, even wisdom. As the disciples were going forth as sheep in the midst of wolves, Jesus counseled them, "Be ye therefore wise as serpents." (Matt. 10:16.)

Those serving the Lord were given "power to tread on serpents and scorpions, and over all the power of the enemy: and nothing shall by any means hurt [them]." (Luke 10:19.) If they happened to touch any serpent or were stung by any scorpion, they were promised no harm. (See Mark 16:18.)

When the Lord sent poisonous serpents among the impatient and rebellious Israelites in the Sinai Wilderness, Moses prayed for the people to be spared. "The Lord said unto Moses, Make thee a fiery serpent, and set it upon a pole: and it shall come to pass, that every one that is bitten, when he looketh upon it, shall live. And Moses made a serpent of brass, and put it upon a pole, and it came to pass, that if a serpent had bitten any man, when he beheld the serpent of brass, he lived." (Num. 21:8–9.)

New Testament writers saw in that event a type or similitude in anticipation of the Messiah: "As Moses lifted up the serpent in the wilderness, even so must the Son of man be lifted up: that whosoever believeth in him should not perish, but have eternal life." (John 3:14–15; see also Alma 33:19–20; Hel. 8:13–15.) As Israel had looked to the serpent on a pole to live, so they were now encouraged to

The land of Israel is on one of the world's major bird migration routes. Here, a Tristram's grackle perches on a ruined wall at Masada near the Dead Sea.

A dove resting on barbed wire in front of "Skull Hill," Jerusalem.

Serpents representing healing power carved into a column at the Asclepieum at Pergamum in the Roman province of Asia.

look to their Redeemer, who would be lifted up and would live. The serpent was apparently a symbol of God.

From the very beginning, however, there was a perversion of the true symbol. Lucifer, or Satan, usurped the image to represent himself. "The great dragon was cast out, that old serpent, called the Devil, and Satan, which deceiveth the whole world." (Rev. 12:9; 20:2.) "The serpent beguiled Eve through his subtilty." (2 Cor. 11:3.)

Moses' serpent on a pole was able to heal; and the Savior lifted up on the cross was able to heal. The snake's healing powers persisted in the mythologies of Near Eastern religions, even down to the Graeco-Roman Asclepius, the god of healing and medicine. Healing or medical centers were established throughout the Roman Empire, for example the Asclepieum at Pergamum and the Asklepeion on the island of Cos (where Hippocrates practiced for many years). The symbol of Asclepius was a serpent wrapped around a pole. Today it is the symbol of the American Medical Association.

The parallel of the serpent with God penetrated other ancient cultures as well. For example, the Aztec god Quetzalcoatl, "Precious Serpent," reputedly lived in Coatzacoalcos, which means "sanctuary of the serpent." To ancient Mesoamericans, the serpent was associated with fertility and wisdom and power. In Baalism, for example, the serpent's role was in stimulating moisture, hence fertility.

There are presently at least thirty-five species of snakes and fifteen species of scorpions in the land of Israel. In comparing the good things that mankind can give to the good gifts God can give, Jesus illustrated from nature: "What man is there of you, whom if his son ask bread, will he give him a stone? Or if he ask a fish, will he give him a serpent?" (Matt. 7:9–10.) "Or if he shall ask an egg, will he offer him a scorpion?" (Luke 11:12.)

Humans generally look upon the world of creeping things as ominous and treacherous, particularly the rapacious reptiles and the alarming arachnids. In the Revelator's eschatological description of the final battle, scorpions represent danger, harm, and pain: "Their torment was as the torment of a scorpion, when he striketh a man." (Rev. 9:5.) "They had tails like unto scorpions, and there were stings in their tails: and their power was to hurt men." (Rev. 9:10.)

*"Where moth . . . doth corrupt . . . "*
*(Matt. 6:19.)*

The mention of moths in the Bible usually refers to the eating of clothes. For instance, James noted the destructive nature of the moth: "Your riches are corrupted, and your garments are motheaten." (James 5:2.)

That reference and the two other New Testament references to moths all point to the transitory nature of worldly wealth. "Lay not up for yourselves treasures upon earth, where moth and rust doth corrupt, and where thieves break through and steal: but lay up for yourselves treasures in heaven, where neither moth nor rust doth corrupt, and where thieves do not break through nor steal." (Matt. 6:19–20.)

"Sell that ye have, and give alms; provide yourselves bags which wax not old, a treasure in the heavens that faileth not, where no thief approacheth, neither moth corrupteth." (Luke 12:33.)

## "His meat was locusts and wild honey." (Matt. 3:4.)

The locust is the most frequently mentioned insect in scripture. Locusts were one of the ten plagues of Egypt, and they have been the periodically recurring plague of the modern Near East and Africa. Major invasions of the desert locust, *Schistocerca gregaria,* have occurred in recent decades, desolating lands of all their vegetation. A swarm of locusts one square mile can devour four hundred tons a day. One recent swarm covered hundreds of square miles and contained an estimated forty billion insects that ate four thousand tons a day, destroying enough food to feed one million people for a year.[2]

The locust was looked upon in ancient Israel as an instrument of God's curse—a punishment for sin: "If ye will not hearken unto me, . . . I will even appoint over you terror. . . . : ye shall sow your seed in vain. . . . And I will bring the land into desolation." (Lev. 26:14, 16, 32.) "Thou shalt carry much seed out into the field, and shalt gather but little in; for the locust shall consume it. . . . All thy trees and fruit of thy land shall the locust consume . . . because thou hearkenedst not unto the voice of the Lord thy God, to keep his commandments." (Deut. 28:38, 42, 45.)

Again, in John's apocalyptic preview of the last great battle, armies were com-pared to hordes of locusts: "There came out of the smoke locusts upon the earth: and unto them was given power, as the scorpions. . . . And the shapes of the locusts were like unto horses prepared unto battle." (Rev. 9:3, 7.)

The diet of John the Baptist in the Judaean Wilderness included locusts and wild honey. We have already seen that some would define locusts as the pods of the carob tree. (See "He would fain have filled his belly with the husks . . . ," in chapter 8.) We cannot exclude, however, the possibility that John ate the actual small insect. Natives of the Near East and Africa even today eat locusts; to some, they are considered a delicacy.

John also ate wild honey. According to the context of some biblical passages and some rabbinic sources, we understand that honey is the thick, heavy syrup of dates or of grapes.[3] (See Gen. 43:11; Ezek. 27:17.) The honey (*dvash*) of the Hebrew Bible may also be the product of bees. The Greek term (*meli*) used in Matthew 3:4 means bee honey, and the honeycomb that was given to Jesus to eat after his resurrection (see Luke 24:42) was a honeycomb from a beehive.

John the Baptist may, therefore, have eaten in the Judaean Wilderness carob pods and date syrup, or insects and bee honey. The former may seem to us more palatable, but the latter are more probable.

## "Ye blind guides, which strain at a gnat, and swallow a camel." (Matt. 23:24.)

The Greek term employed here and translated as "gnat" may also mean mosquito or generally any blood-sucking insect. This hyperbole spoken by Jesus denounced scribes and Pharisees, the would-be guides of their people's spiritual lives. They gave overmuch attention to minute, nagging details of ritual and ceremony (comparable to pesky mosquitos), but at the same time they attempted to incorporate the huge mass of accumulated rabbinic tradition and interpretation (comparable to an entire camel), neglecting the more important, basic laws of justice, mercy, and faith.

### "They stripped him, and put on him a scarlet robe." (Matt. 27:28.)

In the New Testament, we learn of a "scarlet robe" that was placed on Jesus when Roman soldiers mocked him (Matt. 27:26–28), of "scarlet wool" (Heb. 9:19), of a woman sitting on a "scarlet coloured beast" (Rev. 17:3), and of "scarlet colour" or simply "scarlet" (Rev. 17:4; 18:12, 16). The red color is derived from the eggs of an insect (*Coccus ilicis*) that lives in oak trees in the Holy Land. The red derivative is used to dye cloth. The Arabs call it *kirmiz*, which is the source of our English word *crimson*.

Isaiah 1:18 uses the terms scarlet and crimson in parallel to describe the guilt of a sinner: "Though your sins be as scarlet, they shall be as white as snow; though they be red like crimson, they shall be as wool." Scarlet often identified those things that were evil or sinful. However, along with purple dye, scarlet was also symbolic of things royal, thus its use in placing a robe on Jesus, making a mockery of his acclaimed royalty.

### "They clothed him with purple." (Mark 15:17.)

Though Matthew referred to a scarlet robe placed on Jesus, Mark and John wrote that Jesus was clothed with purple. (John 19:2.) Either color served the purpose of ridiculing the Lord. The Roman soldiers then placed a crown of thorns on his head, "and when they had mocked him, they took off the purple from him, and put his own clothes on him, and led him out to crucify him." (Mark 15:20.)

On one occasion earlier, Jesus had related a story about "a certain rich man, which was clothed in purple and fine linen, and fared sumptuously." (Luke 16:19.) Several times in the book of Revelation, purple is included with scarlet and other dyed items to suggest richness, luxury, and royalty. (See 17:4; 18:12, 16.) And a certain woman living in Philippi at the time of Paul was "a seller of purple." (Acts 16:14.)

What is this *purple* spoken of? Israelites, as well as other societies of the ancient Near East, prized the color dyes, blue, scarlet, and purple in particular. As with other elements and composites in nature that are comparatively rare, like gold and diamonds, the dyes were treasured because of the limited quantity available. Purple was extracted by the Phoenicians, especially Tyrians, from Murex snails (part of the mollusk phylum), which thrive along the northeastern Mediterranean coast, and were used in textile-dyeing industries. Recent experiments by marine biologists and chemists in the Near East have established the certain origin of royal

126

purple and the possible origin of biblical blue from the female and male *rock murex*.

## "Give not that which is holy unto the dogs." (Matt. 7:6.)

The above behest was given in a parallelism; the second phrase is "neither cast ye your pearls before swine." The parallel clearly defines the Hebrews' regard for the dog. Unlike in modern Western society, the dog in Israelite culture was not "man's best friend," but rather an ill-respected scavenger. Jesus said, "It is not meet to take the children's bread, and to cast it to dogs" (Matt. 15:26), a hyperbolic statement of the priority of gospel dissemination and of the care with which the mysteries of the kingdom should be reserved for the spiritually attuned.

Figuratively, then, dogs represent unworthy persons. Peter recalled this proverb, which also parallels dogs with swine: "The dog is turned to his own vomit again; and the sow that was washed to her wallowing in the mire." (2 Pet. 2:22.) Paul said simply, "Beware of dogs, beware of evil workers." (Philip. 3:2.)

## "I send you forth as lambs among wolves." (Luke 10:3.)

Wolves also represent unworthy persons, those attempting to destroy the flock of God (his church and its members). "Behold, I send you forth as sheep in the midst of wolves," Jesus told his apostles. (Matt. 10:16.)

All New Testament uses of the wolf are in a figurative context, carrying the deeper, underlying meaning of fierce apostates and antagonists determined to

harm the sheep of his fold. "Beware of false prophets, which come to you in sheep's clothing, but inwardly they are ravening wolves." (Matt. 7:15.) "He that is an hireling, and not the shepherd, whose own the sheep are not, seeth the wolf coming, and leaveth the sheep, and fleeth: and the wolf catcheth them, and scattereth the sheep." (John 10:12.) "For I know this, that after my departing shall grievous wolves enter in among you, not sparing the flock." (Acts 20:29.)

## "The foxes have holes." (Matt. 8:20.)

Disciples of Jesus were told that in following him they would not even have the security and comfort that animals have: the foxes burrow their holes and the birds build their nests, but the disciple, following the example of the Son of Man, may have to abandon permanence and embrace transience. The disciple may be called to forsake the stability of home and travel, without purse or scrip, to minister to the needs of others.

There is no case in the recorded words of Jesus where he ever applied an epithet to any individual, except once. He called Herod Antipas, the tetrarch of Galilee and Peraea, the one who beheaded John the Baptist, "that fox." (Luke 13:32.) The fox in Old Testament and Greek literature represented cunning, craftiness, and destructiveness. In rabbinic literature, the fox stood for the ignominious or contemptuous. Certain Pharisees had come warning Jesus to get out of Antipas' territory because Herod would try to kill him. Jesus' response to the Pharisees clearly signaled his unconcern for Herod's intentions, since Herod could not interrupt his work. He would finish his work there in Peraea and then journey on to Jerusalem, "for it cannot be that a prophet perish out of Jerusalem." (Luke 13:33.)

## "Jonas was three days and three nights in the whale's belly." (Matt. 12:40.)

The book of Jonah records that a "great fish" swallowed Jonah. (1:17.) In Matthew's recounting of the experience, Jesus spoke of the prophet's staying three days and three nights in the belly of a *ketos,* that is, a "great fish" or "sea monster." The King James' translators chose the term *whale,* though there is no way to specifically identify the species of the great fish. It could also have been the common white shark, which is of sufficient size to swallow a man and is known in the Mediterranean.

Two additional points may be made regarding this reference. Since some have labeled the story of Jonah as scriptural fiction, as a fable, we should note that Jesus' mention of the prophet and his unique ordeal, and the fact that the Ninevites "repented at the preaching of Jonas" (Matt. 12:41), gives the whole episode great historical credibility.

Jesus' purpose in alluding to Jonah (Greek, *Jonas*) was to give the scribes and Pharisees "a sign." The sign of the prophet Jonah — his three days and three nights in the belly of the great fish — was a type of things to come: "So shall the Son of man be three days and three nights in the heart of the earth." (Matt. 12:40.) He was, of course, referring to his death, burial, and resurrection. "Three days and three nights" is an idiom covering any parts of three days and nights. At his death Jesus did not literally remain in the earth three whole days and three whole nights, else his rising from the dead would have been on the *fourth* day, whereas the scriptures ten times mention his resurrection "on the third day."

### NOTES

1. *Teachings of the Prophet Joseph Smith,* comp. Joseph Fielding Smith (Salt Lake City: Deseret Book Company, 1976), 275–76.

2. James Hudson, *Rand McNally Illustrated Atlas of the Middle East* (New York: Rand McNally and Company, 1979), 22. See also Alan C. G. Best and Harm J. deBlij, *African Survey* (New York: John Wiley and Sons, 1977), 55.

3. Jerusalem Talmud, *Bikkurim,* 1,3.

# TRADING AND ECONOMY

*"Salutations in the marketplaces . . . "*
*(Mark 12:38.)*

In the New Testament, the words *marketplace* and *market* are the translation of the Greek word *agora*. These English words do not fully convey the function of the agora as a public gathering center for social life as well as a place of commerce or a marketplace.

The agora was usually a large open space near the city center that had three basic functions. It was a commercial center, containing shops, stalls, tradesmen, and merchants. Public buildings such as the city hall, courts, and temples typically surrounded the agora, making it also the municipal center of the city. The third function of the agora was as a place of socializing and recreation. "Whereunto shall I liken this generation? It is like unto children sitting in the markets, and calling unto their fellows, and saying, We have piped [played on a flute] unto you, and ye have not danced." (Matt. 11:16–17.)

The market was the place where scribes and Pharisees would be greeted and called "Rabbi, Rabbi" (Matt. 23:7), and where they would parade their fine clothing. "Beware of the scribes, which love to go in long clothing, and love salutations in the marketplaces." (Mark 12:38.) "Woe unto you, Pharisees! for ye love the uppermost seats in the synagogues, and greetings in the markets." (Luke 11:43.)

The market was also the place where the unemployed sought work and where employers would go to find workers. "For the kingdom of heaven is like unto a man that is an householder, which went out early in the morning to hire labourers into his vineyard. And when he had agreed with the labourers for a penny a day, he sent them into his vineyard. And he went out about the third hour, and saw others standing idle in the marketplace, and said unto them; Go ye also into the vineyard. . . . And he went out about the sixth and ninth hour, and did likewise. And about the eleventh hour he went out, and found others standing idle, and saith unto them, Why stand ye here all day idle? They say unto him, Because no man hath hired us." (Matt. 20:1–7.)

*"Jesus . . . overthrew the tables of the moneychangers." (Matt. 21:12.)*

There are various uses of money mentioned in the New Testament. "Tribute money" was paid to the Roman occupiers. (See Matt. 17:24; 22:19.) "Bribe money" was paid to Roman soldiers to lie about the disappearance of Jesus' body (see Matt. 28:12, 15), and Felix hoped to induce bribe money from Paul to release him (see Acts 24:26). By offering money, Simon the former sorceror hoped to buy priesthood power of God. (See Acts 8:18.) "Betrayal money" was given to Judas Iscariot for his role in the apprehension of Jesus. (See Mark 14:11.)

Missionaries were to take no money in their purses. (See Mark 6:8.) Worshipers deposited their money into the Temple treasury. (See Mark 12:41.) Money was also deposited in banks—that is, with the exchangers to earn "usury," or interest (see Matt. 25:27; Luke 19:23)—or it was used to engage in trading (see Matt. 25:16; Luke 19:15). Church members donated it to the Church, especially for others who needed help. (See Acts 4:37; 11:29–30.)

Despite the good that money could do, the attitude of the early Church about money is reflected in the writings of Paul: "The love of money is the root of all evil: which while some coveted after, they have erred from the faith, and pierced themselves through with many sorrows." (1 Tim. 6:10.) James describes some of those evils associated with money: greed, fraud, and wantonness. (See James 5:1–5.)

Three main currencies were in circulation in the Holy Land during Jesus' lifetime—Roman, Greek, and Jewish. Roman coinage consisted of the copper quadrans (Greek, *kodrantes*) and assarion, the bronze dupondius and sestertius, the silver denarius, and the gold aureus. The quadrans

was the coin of least value—at the time of Jesus, it was worth 1/64 of a denarius. When Jesus sent the Twelve on missions, he instructed them, "Provide neither gold, nor silver, nor brass [copper] in your purses" (Matt. 10:9), probably referring to ordinary Roman coinage.

Jesus mentioned that if a man were sent to prison by his opponent in a law suit, he would not be released until he paid "the uttermost farthing," that is, the last quadrans. (See Matt. 5:25–26.) The word *farthing* is also used in the King James Version for an assarion, which was worth four quadrans. For instance, two sparrows were "sold for a farthing" (Greek, *assarion*). (See Matt. 10:29.)

Laborers in the vineyard earned a denarius (KJV, "penny," plural "pence"), which was a day's wage for the common laborer. (See Matt. 20:1–16.) The Good Samaritan paid the innkeeper two denarii to care for the wounded Jew. (See Luke 10:35.) When asked whether paying tribute to Caesar was lawful, Jesus had a denarius brought to him for an object lesson. (See Matt. 22:17–21.)

Greek coinage included the silver drachma, didrachma, and tetradrachma or stater. The Greek drachma and Roman denarius were equal in value. The mina and talent were sums of money, not single coins. The woman's lost coin was a drachma. (See Luke 15:8.) The coin in the fish's mouth was a stater, which was worth four drachma. (See Matt. 17:27.) A certain nobleman journeying into a far country gave "pounds," or minas, to his servants. (See Luke 19:12–13.) One pound was a sum of coins worth twenty-five sta-

A marketplace in Jerusalem. Even today, the local marketplace is a center not only for commerce, but also for socializing.

Jewish coins from New Testament times. Jewish rulers put such symbols as palm trees, grape leaves, and grape clusters on their coins to avoid making idolatrous graven images, common on Greek and Roman coins.

The outer court, or Court of the Gentiles, is the large spacious area surrounding the Temple proper. This court is where the merchants and moneychangers bought and sold, and this is the court that Jesus cleared twice. (See John 2:13–16; Matt. 21:12–13.) The gate in the foreground is the Susa Gate. From the model city of New Testament Jerusalem at the Holyland Hotel, Jerusalem.

ters. In teaching the Parable of the Talents, Jesus mentioned one, two, and five talents. (See Matt. 25:14–30.) Fifteen hundred staters comprised one talent.

The Roman Empire allowed Jews the privilege of minting their own local coins. The lepton is one Jewish bronze coin mentioned in the New Testament. It was two lepta, or "mites," that the widow deposited in the treasury (see Mark 12:42; Luke 21:2), according to the scripture the equivalent of one quadrans.

The most famous New Testament users of money were the moneychangers. Roman and Greek money was legal tender for secular purposes, but the rabbis and Temple administrators had declared only Jewish and Temple coinage appropriate for sacred functions, thereby setting themselves up for financial profit through the transactions of the changers. According to the law of Moses, every Israelite male over twenty years of age owed a half shekel to the Temple treasury as an offering to Jehovah. (See Ex. 30:12–14.) This had to be changed from the usual foreign currency into currency appropriate for keeping in the Temple, which also served as the economic center of the Jewish people. The Jews determined that the didrachma, or four denarii, was equivalent to the half shekel.

Though upholding the sanctity and legitimacy of the Temple proper, Jesus lashed out against the ill-motivated merchandising and fraudulant profiteering of the moneychangers and the authorities responsible for the changing: "Jesus went into the temple of God, and cast out all them that sold and bought in the temple, and overthrew the tables of the moneychangers, and the seats of them that sold doves, and said unto them, It is written, My house shall be called the house of prayer; but ye have made it a den of thieves." (Matt. 21:12–13.)

*"With what measure ye mete, it shall be measured to you again." (Matt. 7:2.)*

"Give, and it shall be given unto you; good measure, pressed down, and shaken together, and running over, shall men give into your bosom [lap; that is, the outer garment in the lap]. For with the same measure that ye mete withal it shall be measured to you again." (Luke 6:38.)

The New Testament mentions "measures of meal [wheat flour]" (Luke 13:21), "measures of oil" (Luke 16:6), "measures of wheat" (Luke 16:7), and "measures of barley" (Rev. 6:6). A measure is roughly equivalent to a U.S. dry quart and is also translated in the Revised Standard Version as "quart."

A *bushel* was approximately seven and a half dry quarts or a little less than half a U.S. bushel (8.75 liters, or one peck). This grain measure was the object spoken of in the Sermon on the Mount: "Neither do men light a candle, and put it under a bushel, but on a candlestick; and it giveth light unto all that are in the house." (Matt. 5:15.)

*"As many as trade by sea . . ." (Rev. 18:17.)*

Even before the Israelite periods but increasingly in the Hellenistic and Roman periods, sea trade developed into a complex network of commercial traffic lines. Countries of the Levant traded by sea with Egypt and other points in northern Africa, with the Mediterranean islands, and particularly with northern Mediterranean lands and peoples. A flourishing land trade also existed with Nabataeans, Arabians, and Mesopotamians and beyond.

The book of Acts alone records shipping ventures to and from Judaea, Phoenicia and Syria (see 21:2, 3), Asia [Minor], Italy, and Egypt (see 27:2, 6; 28:11). Some of the commodities involved in international trade are noted in the New Testament record.

*"They returned, and prepared spices and ointments." (Luke 23:56.)*

The word for *spice* in Greek is *aroma*. Spices and ointments were usually scented and were used for funerary, cosmetic, and medicinal purposes. They were already in heavy use in Old Testament times. (See, for example, Ex. 30:34–38; Song. 1:12–13; Prov. 7:17; Isa. 57:9; Esth. 2:12.) Every time the word *spice* appears in the New Testament, it refers in some way to Jesus' embalming and burial.

"When the sabbath was past, Mary Magdalene, and Mary the mother of James, and Salome, had bought sweet spices, that they might come and anoint him." (Mark 16:1.) "They returned, and prepared spices and ointments; and rested the sabbath day according to the commandment. . . . Early in the morning, they came unto the sepulchre, bringing the spices which they had prepared." (Luke 23:56–24:1.) "Then took they the body of Jesus, and wound it in linen clothes with the spices, as the manner of the Jews is to bury." (John 19:40.)

The spices used for Jesus' body were a mixture of myrrh and aloes, "about an hundred pound weight." (See John 19:39.) "Pound" is the translation of Greek *litra*, which was actually twelve ounces by U.S. standards. Still, the total mixture amounted to a hefty seventy-five pounds.

*Myrrh* (Hebrew, *mor*) is said to come from the odorous gum of the *Balsamodendron myrrha*, which grew in Arabia, Ethiopia, and India, and also in the Rift Valley of the Holy Land and the Kidron Valley of Jerusalem. It is mentioned three times in the New Testament. Myrrh first appears as one of the gifts of the wise men from the east to the child Jesus and is mentioned among two other costly gifts, gold and frankincense. (See Matt. 2:11.) According to Mark's account, wine "mingled [mixed or flavored] with myrrh" was offered to Jesus on the cross, possibly as a pain killer, but "he received it not." (Mark 15:23.)

There is a variety of plants in the *aloe* family, some used for medicinal purposes, others for fragrant perfumes. We do not know exactly which specific aloes were brought for Jesus' burial, but those used for his embalmment may have come from the oil extracted from the aloe vera plant, which was used in ancient Egypt and elsewhere in the Old World for embalming.

The spice *spikenard* is mentioned twice. Spikenard was a costly, scented ointment imported from the Himalayas. A pound of pure spikenard could be sold for over three hundred denarii, the better part of a year's wages. Its costliness is expressed emphatically by the petulance of those present when a woman anointed Jesus with the precious ointment: "Being in Bethany in the house of Simon the leper, as [Jesus] sat at meat, there came a woman having an alabaster box of ointment of spikenard very precious; and she brake the box, and poured it on his head. And there were some that had indignation within themselves, and said, Why was this waste of the ointment made? For it might have been sold for more than three hundred pence [denarii], and have been given to the poor. And they murmured against her. And Jesus said, Let her alone. . . . She is come aforehand to anoint my body to the burying." (Mark 14:3-8.)

The spice *frankincense* (Hebrew, *levonah*) is mentioned twice, once, as before mentioned, as one of the gifts of the wise men to Jesus. (See Matt. 2:11.) Revelation 18:13 refers to it again as one of the products traded into "Babylon," which some have interpreted as Rome. Frankincense comes from the *Boswellia* tree that grew in South Arabia, East Africa, and India. It was imported to the land of Israel often by camel caravans from Sheba. (See Isa. 60:6.)

The general term *ointment* is a translation of the Greek word *muron*, signifying perfumed oil or salve. The word *muron* is related to the word *myrrh,* this spice being used frequently in ointments. Olive oil was usually used as the base for ointments, to which spices like myrrh and spikenard were added. (See Ex. 30:23–25.) In Jesus' day, ointments were commonly stored in alabaster boxes or jars.

*"The kingdom of heaven is like unto a merchant man, seeking goodly pearls." (Matt. 13:45.)*

References to pearls in the Bible are found almost exclusively in the New Testament. They are the only gem created by a living process and are found at sea. Thus they were imported into the land of Israel. Pearls always represent richness and luxury and are listed with other precious commodities in several passages.

Jesus taught that it would be worth all else a person owns to search out and purchase one pearl of great price: meaning the kingdom of God. (See Matt. 13:46.) The gates of the New Jerusalem were described as twelve pearls. (See Rev. 21:21.) The delicate structure of pearls is implied in Jesus' warning not to cast pearls before swine (see Matt. 7:6), since, unlike the harder gems, pearls are relatively soft and trampling on them could destroy them.

# JERUSALEM AND THE TEMPLE

*"Jerusalem . . . the city of the great King . . . " (Matt. 5:35.)*

To the Christian, the greatest events in history took place in Jerusalem: the atoning sacrifice and resurrection of the Lord Jesus. To Jew and Christian, Jerusalem is closest to the celestial realms of God. When he chose to visit his people, he came to Jerusalem. His dwelling place was there. His meeting place was there. His glory filled his House. He manifested himself to his servants, the prophets. For a millennium, he was worshipped in Jerusalem. His people "looked for redemption in Jerusalem." (Luke 2:38.) From Melchizedek to Malachi, the Messiah was anticipated and announced.

Jesus clearly knew the importance Jerusalem would have in his mission. "When the time was come that he should be received up, he stedfastly set his face to go to Jerusalem" (Luke 9:51), "for" as Jesus noted, "it cannot be that a prophet perish out of Jerusalem" (Luke 13:33). He told his disciples, "We go up to Jerusalem, and all things that are written by the prophets concerning the Son of man shall be accomplished." (Luke 18:31.) "From that time forth began Jesus to shew unto

his disciples, how that he must go unto Jerusalem, and suffer many things of the elders and chief priests and scribes, and be killed, and be raised again the third day" (Matt. 16:21.)

Jesus wept over the city as he recalled her past and foreshadowed her future. He left no doubt concerning the immediate future of Jerusalem. His were vivid prophetic but pathetic pronouncements about the next generations: "Jesus turning unto them said, Daughters of Jerusalem, weep not for me, but weep for yourselves, and for your children." (Luke 23:28.) "Ye shall see Jerusalem compassed with armies, then know that the desolation thereof is nigh. . . . And they shall fall by the edge of the sword, and shall be led away captive into all nations: and Jerusalem shall be trodden down of the Gentiles." (Luke 21:20, 24.)

What was it all for? Why would Jesus and Jerusalem both suffer indignities and anguish and death? Their end was but a beginning. Jesus and Jerusalem would resurrect and live again. Both must be buried and brought forth anew. John the Revelator saw the glory of that day:

"I John saw the holy city, new Jeru-

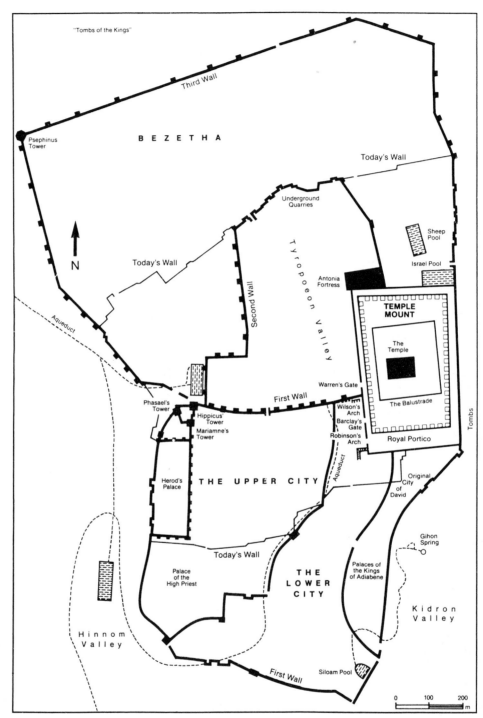

"Tombs of the Kings"

Third Wall

BEZETHA

Psephinus Tower

Today's Wall

Today's Wall

Underground Quarries

Sheep Pool

Israel Pool

Second Wall

Tyropoeon Valley

Antonia Fortress

TEMPLE MOUNT

The Temple

The Balustrade

Aqueduct

N

Warren's Gate

First Wall

Wilson's Arch

Barclay's Gate

Robinson's Arch

Royal Portico

Tombs

Phasael's Tower

Hippicus' Tower

Mariamne's Tower

Aqueduct

Original City of David

Herod's Palace

THE UPPER CITY

Gihon Spring

Today's Wall

Palace of the High Priest

THE LOWER CITY

Palaces of the Kings of Adiabene

Kidron Valley

Hinnom Valley

First Wall

Siloam Pool

0   100   200
m

Map 4
Jerusalem during the time of Herod's Temple.

salem, coming down from God out of heaven, prepared as a bride adorned for her husband. And I heard a great voice out of heaven, saying, Behold, the tabernacle of God is with men, and he will dwell with them, and they shall be his people, and God himself shall be with them, and be their God. And God shall wipe away all tears from their eyes; and there shall be no more death, neither sorrow, nor crying, neither shall there be any more pain: for the former things are passed away.

"And I saw no temple therein: for the Lord God Almighty and the Lamb are the temple of it. And the city had no need of the sun, neither of the moon, to shine in it: for the glory of God did lighten it, and the Lamb is the light thereof. And the nations of them which are saved shall walk in the light of it: and the kings of the earth do bring their glory and honour into it." (Rev. 21:2–4, 22–24.)

## "Jesus went unto the mount of Olives." (John 8:1.)

The mile-long Mount of Olives range lies to the east of the most ancient parts of Jerusalem. Its distance from the city is given in the New Testament: "The mount called Olivet . . . is from Jerusalem a sabbath day's journey"—that is, about three thousand feet. (Acts 1:12; see "But they . . . went a day's journey," chapter 1.)

The Mount of Olives may be divided into three sections. The northernmost section was called by Josephus and is still called today Mount Scopus (Greek, *scopos,* meaning lookout point), where Babylon-

ian and Roman armies camped and watched the city they were besieging. The Hebrew name of Mount Scopus is *Har HaTsofim,* meaning the mount of watchmen. The whole of the Mount of Olives is certainly a watchtower over Jerusalem, a guardian especially of the holy Temple Mount below.

The middle and southern sections, east and southeast of the Temple Mount, are today called the Mount of Olives, although the southernmost section, directly east of the ancient City of David, was in Old Testament times also known as the Mount of Scandal, the Mount of Offense, or the "mount of corruption" (2 Kgs. 23:13) because of the shrines that Solomon allowed to be erected there for his wives' idol gods (see 1 Kgs. 11:7–8).

Today the midsouthern portion of the Mount of Olives is a cemetery, one of the oldest, continuously used cemeteries in the world. Already by Jesus' day, thousands of tombs had been cut in the soft chalky limestone (from the Senonian period—more easily cut than the harder Turonian and Cenomanian limestones to the west). Hundreds of tombs from the period of the Old Testament have now been investigated by archaeologists, and many hundreds of ossuaries (small stone boxes for reburial of bones) have been uncovered from the New Testament period. There are presently over seventy thousand graves visible on the Mount of Olives.

Jewish traditions have encouraged the pious to hope for burial on the Mount of Olives in order to be part of the first resurrection when the Messiah comes. Indeed, according to Christian scripture, some disciples have already risen from that cemetery: "The graves were opened; and many bodies of the saints which slept arose, and came out of the graves after his resurrection, and went into the holy city, and appeared unto many." (Matt. 27:52–53.)

The Mount of Olives is mentioned frequently in the Gospels in connection with the towns of Bethany and Bethphage on its eastern slopes and because of places on the mount where Jesus taught and prayed. "As he sat upon the mount of Olives over against the temple, Peter and James and John and Andrew asked him privately, "Tell us, when shall these things be?" (Mark 13:3.) "He came out, and went, as he was wont [accustomed], to the mount of Olives; and his disciples also followed him." (Luke 22:39.) "Jesus ofttimes resorted thither with his disciples." (John 18:2.)

In his triumphal entry into the city, Jesus came from the east, beginning on the eastern side of the Mount of Olives: "When he was come nigh, even now at the descent of the mount of Olives, the whole multitude of the disciples began to rejoice and praise God with a loud voice for all the mighty works that they had seen." (Luke 19:37.)

The Mount of Olives is where Jesus descended below all men (the Atonement) and where he ascended above all men (the Ascension). With his mortal work finished, Jesus departed into heaven from this eastern mountain of Jerusalem. (Luke 24:51.) His return in the end of time will be to the same Mount: "When he had spoken these things, while they beheld, he

was taken up; and a cloud received him out of their sight. And while they looked stedfastly toward heaven as he went up, behold, two men stood by them in white apparel; which also said, Ye men of Galilee, why stand ye gazing up into heaven? this same Jesus, which is taken up from you into heaven, shall so come in like manner as ye have seen him go." (Acts 1:9–11; see also v. 12.)

*"Go, wash in the pool of Siloam."*
*(John 9:7.)*

During the Second Temple Period, Jerusalem enjoyed highly developed water resources. Wells, springs, cisterns, aqueducts, and pools were all in operation to service the water needs of one of the greatest walled cities in the Near East. Moving water — groundwater and water transported via aqueduct — was the best quality water, since open pools have the natural disadvantages of heavy evaporation, silting, and exposure to sewage and other pollutants. Notwithstanding the disadvantages, Jerusalem featured at least ten pools in this period. Two are mentioned in the New Testament.

Jesus one day sent a man blind from birth to the Pool of Siloam. He answered the man's plea for sight by making a clay paste, applying it to his eyes, and instructing him to go to the pool and wash it off. The blind man obeyed and was healed. (See John 9:1–11.)

The Pool of Siloam stands at the end of the ancient city's most unique hydrotechnical project: Hezekiah's Tunnel. In the year 701 B.C., King Hezekiah, encouraged by the lone voice of the prophet Isa-

*Top left:* Over seventy thousand graves are visible on the Mount of Olives. *Top right:* This nineteenth-century photograph shows some impressive burial monuments from the Hellenistic and early Roman periods at the lower slope of the Mount of Olives. *Center left:* The Russian Orthodox Tower of Ascension marks the traditional site where Jesus ascended into heaven from the Mount of Olives. *Center right:* The Pool of Siloam (left of center, with colonnades on four sides), as seen in the model city of ancient Jerusalem at the Holyland Hotel, Jerusalem. *Bottom left:* The probable sites of the Last Supper and the palace of Caiaphas (palacial complex, left of the pyramidal structure) were in this section of Jerusalem, as seen in the model city. *Bottom right:* The Garden of Gethsemane, photographed in 1870.

iah, prepared for the attack of the Assyrian king Sennacherib's forces by repairing the city walls and carving out of solid limestone an underground water channel nearly eighteen hundred feet long, in order to camouflage the Gihon Spring, the city's main water source, and bring its waters inside the city for safe access. By Jesus' day, the pool at the south end had provided water storage for seven centuries.

"Now there is at Jerusalem by the sheep market a pool, which is called in the Hebrew tongue Bethesda, having five porches." (John 5:2.) The double pool called the Pool of Bethesda (or Bethzatha—possibly from Aramaic "House of Mercy") was situated just north of the Temple Mount gate called in Greek *probatike* (pertaining to sheep), the gate through which sheep are supposed to have been brought into the Temple for sacrifice.

There were five porticoes, or porches, surrounding the twin pools: four around the sides and one dividing them. Certain medicinal or curative properties were ascribed to the pool. A superstitious tradition had an angel coming down and "troubling" the waters—probably the result of a siphon-karst spring flowing into the pool, causing bubbling at the surface. At this pool, Jesus met an invalid man, lame or paralyzed for thirty-eight years. On the Sabbath day, he raised him up, completely healed. (See John 5:1–16.)

" . . . *in danger of hell fire.*" (*Matt. 5:22.*)

In the Old Testament, the Hebrew word *sheol* is translated "grave," "hell," and occasionally "pit." The scriptural context clearly requires its association with the state and position of the dead who have departed the earth, and it does not mean the future place of punishment, which is our usual definition of *hell*. One of the Greek terms often translated in the New Testament as "hell" is *hades,* a word with pagan origins. But *hades* carries the same meaning as the Hebrew *sheol:* the place where the dead temporarily reside, awaiting resurrection.

The hell to which people are cast down or cast out, the place of punishment by ever-burning fire, is represented by the Greek word *Gehenna.* Gehenna is a Greek transliteration of the Hebrew *Gei Hinnom,* the Valley of Hinnom (or the full name, the Valley of the Son of Hinnom).

The Hinnom Valley was the designated borderline between the tribes of Judah and Benjamin. (See Josh. 15:8; 18:16.) The valley lay to the southwest just outside of the original Zion, the City of David. It lies below what is today called Mount Zion. Centuries before the Roman period, the Hinnom Valley was used for the burning of incense (see 2 Chr. 28:3) and for burning children as sacrifice to idol gods (see 2 Kgs. 23:10; 2 Chr. 33:6; Jer. 7:31). Prophets warned of fiery judgments upon all those involved in such repulsive practices.

The valley was also named "Tophet," possibly deriving from an Aramaic term meaning place of fire. (See Isa. 30:33.) The burning came to be symbolic in the New Testament of the devouring fire of judgment, representing the concept of hell as a place of continual burnings and eternal punishment. The book of Revelation describes hell as a lake of fire and brimstone. (See "A lake of fire burning with brimstone . . . ," chapter 6.)

There are twelve occurrences of Gehenna, translated as "hell" or "hell fire." The most famous is Jesus' teaching in the Sermon on the Mount: "I say unto you, That whosoever is angry with his brother without a cause shall be in danger of the judgment: and whosoever shall say to his brother, Raca [Hebrew and Aramaic, *reyk*, meaning empty, vain, worthless], shall be in danger of the council [Greek, Sanhedrin]: but whosoever shall say, Thou fool, shall be in danger of hell fire [Hebrew, *esh Gei Hinnom*, literally "fire of the Hinnom Valley," or Greek, *Gehenna*]." (Matt. 5:22.)

Another burial place has been associated since early centuries A.D. with the southern slopes of the Hinnom Valley: "It was known unto all the dwellers at Jerusalem; insomuch as that field is called in their proper tongue, Aceldama, that is to say, The field of blood." (Acts 1:19.)

According to Acts 1:18, Judas Iscariot (Hebrew, *ish Kerioth* = man from Kerioth, a Judean village) had purchased with his betrayal money a field that was to be the scene of his suicide. Matthew 27:5–7, on the other hand, preserves the account of Judas casting down the coins in the Temple and going out and hanging himself, whereupon the chief priests bought with the money "the potter's field, to bury strangers in. Wherefore that field was called, The field of blood." Greek *Akeldama* is transliterated from the Aramaic *khakel dema* (field of blood). According to

the New Testament record, then, the renaming of this burial ground in Jerusalem had its origin in the betrayal of Jesus and the death of Judas Iscariot.

*"A large upper room furnished and prepared . . . " (Mark 14:15.)*

We begin our geographical survey of the last week of Jesus' life at the "Upper Room." The longest and strongest traditions indicate that the house containing the Upper Room was located on the hill today called "Mount Zion." That room was where Jesus celebrated the Passover meal with his apostles, where he instituted the sacrament (see Matt. 26:26–29; Luke 22:15–20), where he gave special meaning to the washing of feet (see John 13:2–17), and where he revealed who would betray him (see Matt. 26:20–25; John 13:18–30).

In finding the guest chamber, Jesus instructed Peter and John to follow a *man* bearing a pitcher of water from the Gihon Spring or the Pool of Siloam. Because women usually did the water-carrying, some suppose that this man may have been part of the semi-monastic Essene community that was known to have resided in that part of the Upper City. The apostles proceeded as Jesus had directed and made final preparations for celebrating the Passover—according to John, a day earlier than the community at large, since by sundown on Friday evening Jesus, as the Passover Lamb, would have been sacrificed at the same time as the Passover lamb on the Temple altar and would be in the tomb. (See John 13:1; 18:28; 19:14.)

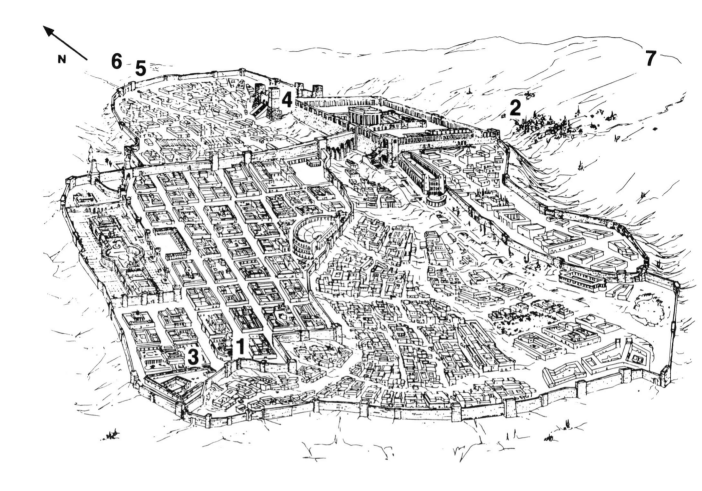

## Map 5

The last week of Jesus' life. (1) Upper Room—the Last Supper. (2) Garden of Gethsemane—the Atonement. (3) The palace of Caiaphas—the Jewish "trial." (4) Antonia Fortress—the Roman "trial." (5) Golgotha, or Calvary—the Crucifixion. (6) The garden tomb for Jesus' burial—the Resurrection. (7) Mount of Olives—the Ascension.

The Upper Room may have been prearranged by Jesus, or else he knew the place by visionary power. It was a furnished room (Greek, *estromenon*, specifically referring to a feast or festival setting); that is, it contained rugs and pillows to recline on for the meal. The room likely included a *triclinium*: a U-shaped, low-lying table around which persons reclined with their feet toward the outside.

If this Upper Room is the same chamber where the resurrected Jesus appeared to many disciples (see Luke 24:36–49) or where the apostles and a hundred others were met to fill the vacancy in the quorum of the Twelve Apostles (see Acts 1:13–26), then it may be the home of John Mark's mother, which served as a meeting place for the followers of Jesus after the Crucifixion (see Acts 12:12).

When Jesus and the eleven apostles had concluded their early observance of the Passover — the last legitimate Passover in history — and after he had given his farewell instructions about unity, love, and the Holy Spirit to his closest associates, "he went forth with his disciples over the brook Cedron, where was a garden, into the which he entered." (John 18:1.)

The Kidron (New Testament, Cedron) is a wadi that begins about a mile north of the Temple Mount and turns southward to run between the Mount of Olives and the Temple Mount, continuing past the former City of David where it joins its tributaries, the Tyropoeon and Hinnom, and then flows southeastward for twenty miles through the Judaean Desert to the Dead Sea.

*"They came to a place which was named Gethsemane." (Mark 14:32.)*

On the slope of the Mount of Olives was a garden area to which Jesus liked to retire for meditation and prayer. "Jesus ofttimes resorted thither with his disciples." (John 18:2.) The garden was appropriately named *Gat Shemen*, which in Hebrew means oil press. Just as the blood (juice) of the grape or olive is pressed and crushed by the heavy stone in the press, so the heavy burden of the sins of the world that was Jesus' to carry would press the blood out of the body of this Anointed One. In Gethsemane, among the olive trees, which were themselves symbolic of the people of Israel, was accomplished along with its consummation at Golgotha, the most selfless suffering in the history of humankind.

Rather than the small area now enclosed by the walls, which surround the Franciscan property that includes the Basilica of the Agony, the Garden of Gethsemane must have extended a considerable distance up the slope of the Mount of Olives. Upon entering the garden, Jesus left eight of his apostles to watch and pray, and he continued farther inside — meaning up the slope — with Peter, James, and John. He then left those three to watch and pray, while he hiked "a stone's cast" (Matt. 26:36–39; Luke 22:41) beyond them.

Following Jesus' agony in Gethsemane, a multitude consisting of chief priests, elders, and soldiers arrived seeking his arrest. At their head was Judas, who kissed Jesus profusely (according to the emphatic form of the Greek verb used in Mark 14:45), greatly confusing the emotions of the moment with a false display of affection.

When the mob's intention was known, Peter stepped forward, swung his sword, and cut off the ear of the high priest's servant. (See John 18:10.) What was Peter doing with a sword? At Passover time, many tens of thousands of people flocked to Jerusalem, more than could be housed inside the walls. Crowds of pilgrims would have camped as close outside the city as possible. In the darkness of the night, a sword might offer some security. When the arresting party arrived with "lanterns and torches and weapons" (John 18:3), some disciples ventured, "Shall we smite with the sword?" (Luke 22:49), possibly intending to defend themselves, or still expecting Jesus to assume the popular view of the Messiah as the one who would overthrow his adversaries and establish a glorious new Jewish kingdom (cf. Luke 24:21; Acts 1:6).

" . . . the palace of the high priest, who was called Caiaphas." (Matt. 26:3.)

Quirinius, the legate of Syria who had conducted a census at the establishment of Judaea as a province, also established Ananus (Hanan, or Annas in the New Testament) as the high priest in Jerusalem. The influential family of Annas would virtually monopolize that office for the succeeding thirty-five years. The high priests were drawn from the narrow Sadducean circle and were regarded by Roman governors as their immediate intermediaries in dealing with the Jewish subjects.

The first Roman praefect, or governor, nominated by the Emperor Tiberius was Valerius Gratus. Gratus was the ruler who appointed Joseph Caiaphas to the priestly hierarchy; and Caiaphas, who was a son-in-law of Annas (see John 18:13), cooperated with Annas in laying down religious policy. Caiaphas remained in office through the long terms of both Valerius Gratus and Pontius Pilate (thus A.D. 18–36) and was therefore involved in the Sanhedrin trial of Jesus.

The palace of Caiaphas was situated either on the summit of today's Mount Zion, just outside the Zion Gate in the Armenian cemetery, or else down the slope a hundred meters on the grounds of St. Peter in Gallicantu (Latin, meaning cockcrow). At the latter site, excavating uncovered a complete set of Jewish weights and measures, possibly indicating judicial purposes. Also, a large lintel inscription was found featuring the Hebrew word *corban* (offering), suggesting that the residents served in priestly functions.

At the palace, some of the Sanhedrin convened illegally for Jesus' trial. Jewish law forbade a court to sit at night and before the preparation day of the high Holy Day. In the porch, or colonnaded courtyard, of this palace (see Matt. 26:71), Peter denied knowing Jesus as he warmed himself at a fire during the early morning hours (see Luke 22:55–62; John 18:15–18).

"Then led they Jesus from Caiaphas unto the hall of judgment." (John 18:28.)

At the northwestern corner of the Temple Mount stood the massive governmental and military headquarters called the Antonia Fortress, constructed by the Hasmonaeans and reconstructed and fortified by Herod and named after Mark Antony. The fortress was called in the New Testament the *Praetorium* (see Mark 15:16), which is a Latin term for the palace with its hearing room to which the Roman governor came to transact public business. As the subhead indicates, it is also called the "hall of judgment." "It was early; and they themselves [Jesus' accusers] went not into the judgment hall, lest they should be defiled; but that they might eat the passover." (John 18:28; see 18:33; 19:9; Acts 23:35.)

Jesus' trial before the Roman governor Pontius Pilatus likely took place in the Antonia Fortress, in the hall of judgment, on what John called "the Pavement, but in the Hebrew, Gabbatha." (John 19:13.) The Hebrew (or Aramaic) Gabbatha is equivalent to the Greek *lithostroton,* meaning the stone courtyard of the judgment hall. Under today's Sisters of Zion Convent may be seen some large Roman flagstones from the time of Hadrian's Aelia Capitolina, nearly a century after Jesus but similar to what must have existed in Herod's former fortress. In the same hall of judgment was Pilate's judgment seat (Greek, *bema*), a raised platform resembling a throne where the governor sat in judgment. "When Pilate therefore heard that saying, he brought Jesus forth, and sat down in the judgment seat." (John 19:13.)

Though some have proposed that the Roman military presence would have been housed in barracks at Herod's palace on the west side of the city, a substantial contingent of soldiers was likely stationed at the Antonia, the biggest fortress in Jerusalem, to keep watch over the Temple Mount, which was the soldiers' main reason for being in Jerusalem. Later, we find Roman soldiers, then Temple guards taking Paul down to the Sanhedrin at their meeting hall in the Temple and returning with him back up into the fortress, called also "the castle." (See Acts 21:34, 37; 22:24; 23:10.) In addition, note that after Pilate listened to Jesus, he sent him to Herod Antipas, who had also come to Jerusalem for the Passover. While Pilate was at the Antonia, Herod was possibly staying at his father's palace on the other side of the city.

The accusation brought against Jesus when arraigned before some of the Sanhedrin was blasphemy—claiming to be God or insulting or violating the sanctity of God, the greatest crime in Jewish law. Romans cared little about the God of the Jews; they themselves had numerous gods whom they cursed at will. However, there was an accusation that was indeed serious enough to cause the governor to arise out of bed very early in the morning to hear—sedition against the Roman government.

In fact, the chief reason Pilate had come up to Jerusalem from his usual residence in Caesarea on the coast was to keep his Roman eye on the Temple Mount, the traditional focus of would-be insurrection and any initiatives to independence. Pilate had already viciously dealt before this date with several messianic revolutionary movements. Jewish leaders were anxious to see the popular preacher Jesus disposed of and were interested in passing the responsibility for his elimination onto the Romans, so they sought Roman sentence to inflict the death penalty. The charge was shifted from blasphemy to treason. (See Luke 23:1–2.)

Though Jews would normally not resent active hostility against the Romans, in this case they would press the charge that Jesus was conspiring to become king of the Jews and was, therefore, a threat to Caesar (as well as to the comfortable position of the Sadducees and high priests who held their positions by the good graces of the Romans). Jewish accusers even went so far as to charge Pilate with being no friend of Caesar if he allowed Jesus' dismissal. (See John 19:12.)

Pilate tried several means to placate the Jews. He proposed to release one notable prisoner for the festival: Barabbas or Jesus. (See Matt. 27:15–18; John 18:39–40.) There seems to be some relation between the names. Barabbas was a revolutionist who may have appropriated a messianic title: his name means "son of the father," whereas Jesus claimed to actually be the "Son of the Father." Pilate also attempted to appease his Jewish constituents by scourging Jesus—flogging him with a leather whip containing jagged pieces of stone, metal, or bone—thus hoping to satisfy the accusers. (See Luke 23:16; John 19:1–5.)

With no reliable witnesses and on the testimony of the accused alone, despite Pilate's inclination to acquit Jesus due to lack of evidence (see Luke 23:4, 15, 22; John 18:38; 19:4, 6), and despite Pilate's own suspicion of the Jewish accusers' motives (see Matt. 27:18), Jesus was ordered to be executed by crucifixion, the usual method of execution for a noncitizen. (Tradition claims that Peter later would also be crucified, though Paul, a Roman citizen, would be beheaded.)

*"The place . . . called Calvary, there they crucified him." (Luke 23:33.)*

The King James Version of Luke identifies the place of Jesus' execution as Calvary, whereas the other three Gospel writers call the place Golgotha: "He bearing his cross went forth into a place called the place of a skull, which is called in the Hebrew Golgotha." (John 19:17.) All four writers associated the execution site with a skull. Hebrew *gulgoleth* and Aramaic *gulgutha* mean skull. Luke's term *Calvary* is actually not a toponym; it is the Latin translation of the Greek *kranion*, which also means skull. (Luke 23:33 reads from the Greek: "When they were come to the place, which is called *kranion*, there they crucified him.")

To what does the skull refer? The site could have had the physical appearance of a skull, or the name could have derived from the place's long-standing use for executions. It probably involves the fact that it was also a place of burial. John 19:17 in the Joseph Smith Translation indicates that Jesus was taken "into a place called the *place of a burial;* which is called in the Hebrew Golgotha." (Italics added.)

*"In the place where he was crucified there was a garden; and in the garden a new sepulchre." (John 19:41.)*

As with other events during the last days of Jesus, there are two major can-

146

didates for the location of the crucifixion, burial, and resurrection. According to scripture and Jewish customs, the site must meet certain conditions:

1. It must be outside the city walls. (See John 19:20.)

2. It must be near a main thoroughfare. (See Matt. 27:39; Mark 15:29; John 19:20.)

3. It must be a place of execution. (See Mark 15:27; Luke 23:33.)

4. There must be a garden nearby. (See John 19:41; 20:15.)

5. The garden must contain at least one tomb (the tomb was therefore nearby the place of crucifixion). (See John 19:41–42.)

6. The rock tomb must be newly cut. (See Matt. 27:60; Luke 23:53; John 19:41.)

7. The tomb apparently had an anteroom (mourning chamber) and several places for burial; the tomb must be large enough to walk into. (See Mark 16:5; Luke 24:3; John 20:8.)

8. This particular tomb must have a large, heavy stone to seal the entrance, with a groove or trough for the stone to roll. (See Matt. 27:60; Mark 15:46; 16:4; Luke 24:2.)

9. The tomb entrance must be small, so that one has to stoop to look inside; a person looking in from the outside could see the place where the body was laid. (See Luke 24:12; John 20:5, 11–12.)

10. The tomb must have some place where linen burial cloths could lie and where a "young man" could sit (Mark 16:5), or where two angels could sit, one at the head and one at the foot of where Jesus' body had lain (see John 20:6–7, 12).

Considering all of the above conditions, we may examine the two traditional options for the site of the crucifixion, burial, and resurrection.

Site one: The Church of the Holy Sepulchre has long been the traditional site of these venerated events. In the fourth century A.D., Constantine's mother Helena made her pilgrimage to the Holy Land and identified the spot, which had had a pagan temple built over it. Recent excavations seem to show that the site, though now within the walls of the Old City of Jerusalem, was outside the walls in Jesus' day. Its location just outside the western city wall could have provided a busy thoroughfare for travelers. There is no evidence that it was a place of execution. There is no evidence of a garden in the vicinity. A stone quarry existed at the Holy Sepulchre site in the first century A.D.

Roman-period tombs have been discovered in the bedrock below the church. They are *kokhim,* the typical style of sepulchre from that period, rock-cut burial niches with enough space for a single body to be inserted. There would be room for someone to walk into the entry chamber of the tomb. There is no evidence that large stones could be rolled to seal the entrance. The condition that most precludes the Holy Sepulchre site is the lack of a bench or shelf on which a body could be placed or on which someone could sit inside the sepulchre. Two angels could in no fashion situate themselves inside a *kokh,* where Jesus' body would have lain.

Site two: The other site hallowed as a possibility is the Garden Tomb, just outside (north) of the Damascus Gate of today's Old City. This tomb, discovered only last century, is now a place of pilgrimage for many thousands of Christians, including some Catholics who would like to see "how it might have been." This site was outside the walls of the city in Jesus' day. It was definitely alongside a main thoroughfare. It appears to have been a place of execution, because today's Damascus Gate was often called "St. Stephen's Gate" during the first millennium A.D., suggesting that Stephen was killed in this same area. St. Stephen's Church, from the fifth century A.D., is immediately north of this site. One of ancient Jerusalem's biggest cisterns and a winepress identify the grounds as a possible garden at that time.

Many tombs have been discovered in the vicinity, most of them dating to the seventh and eighth centuries B.C. The Garden Tomb itself appears to be part of a complex of Judaean period tombs, and most of the complex lies to the north of the Garden Tomb in the property of the École Biblique, the French School of Archaeology. These tombs, unlike the later kokhim, are chambers with side rooms branching off in several directions, each containing usually three benches on which bodies were placed and featuring repositories for bones underneath one of the benches in each room, suggesting perpetual use of the tombs over many generations. Tombs were reused many times in antiquity.

A "new tomb" could also mean a newly remodeled tomb, never used in the newly cut form. The Garden Tomb is nearly identical in style to these older tombs, but has some features of later styles. There is no repository for bones,

and no evidence that it was used many times. It does have more than one room and is large enough to walk into. Though there is no stone at its entrance, the trough for rolling one into place is clearly visible. The original entrance was short enough to require stooping to enter. And there was a bench or shelf (before Byzantine-period architects or others later carved out a sarcophagus) on which burial clothes could have lain and on which angels could have sat, even on the *right side* upon entering. (See Mark 16:5.)

Some have objected to the Garden Tomb as the burial place of Jesus because, by its structural design, it appears strictly related to the style used seven or eight centuries earlier. There are tombs from the early Roman period, however, that combine both old Judaean- and Roman-period styles. At Khirbet Midras in the Shephelah, for example, is a tomb complex dating to the first century B.C. that has the older-style chambers containing benches but also features the later *kokhim*, or niches, and sarcophagi and ossuaries. Even the St. Etienne tomb complex, of which the Garden Tomb seems to be a part, has a chamber with sarcophagi—quite distinct from the other chambers.

Of our two candidates, the enduring reverence of tradition favors the Holy Sepulchre site, but the Garden Tomb more completely fulfills the scriptural conditions listed previously. Still, we do not dogmatically acclaim the one over the other. There is presently no way to know if one of these two sites or yet another site was used for Jesus' burial. Regardless of investigations and evidences and surmises and conclusions, affixing faith to a particular site is not wise. Belief is beyond physical territory. To the Christian the most important message is, "He is risen; he is not here." (Mark 16:6.)

## "God will provide himself a lamb." (Gen. 22:8.)

In addition to all the above, a more theological or philosophical reason may be advanced for looking to the *north* for the place where Jesus' sacrifice occurred. Two millennia earlier, Abraham had made the long, strenuous trek (fifty-three miles uphill, for a man over a hundred years of age) from Beersheba to the mount of Moriah, later to be known as the Temple Mount. (See 2 Chr. 3:1.) He knew how repulsive human sacrifice was and how foreign such a practice is to the true worship of God, yet the command had been given to sacrifice his son.

The test was perfectly designed for Abraham. He had waited so many years for his and Sarah's most precious blessing—that covenant son whom he loved. Now the Lord called on him to sacrifice, to give up, that beloved son. Paul wrote that "by faith Abraham, when he was tried, offered up Isaac: and he that had received the promises offered up his only begotten son." (Heb. 11:17.)

Abraham was going to learn to a degree the magnitude of the sacrifice that God the Father made in giving up his Beloved Son. Abraham's offering of his son Isaac was a similitude of God offering his only Begotten Son. And both may have been accomplished at the same location. By following the Mount of Moriah north-ward to just outside the Second Wall of the city, we see a prominence where the Garden Tomb and other nearby tombs are situated, which was apparently a site of execution and burial in antiquity.

When Abraham and Isaac approached Moriah, Isaac reminded his father that they had the wood for the sacrifice but asked where the sacrifice was. Abraham prophetically responded, "My son, God [*Elohim* in the Hebrew text] will provide himself a lamb." (Gen. 22:7–8.) When Abraham's test was consummated and the angel of the Lord stopped the sacrifice of the son, a ram (not a *lamb*) was substituted. But two thousand years later, perhaps on the northern extension of the same mountain, God did provide a lamb—the Lamb of God was sacrificed. (Note that when a lamb was slain on the great altar of the Temple, it was slain on the *north* side of the altar—see Lev. 1:11.)

Abraham knew something of the meaning of his similitude-sacrifice. He had uttered prophetically—not unintentionally or accidentally—that God would provide a lamb as a sacrifice, and he knew that the Son would be that sacrifice, to be made at that very place (the reason for the long trek to Moriah instead of some hill in the Negev). Jesus said in the Temple itself, "Your father Abraham rejoiced to see my day: and he saw it, and was glad." (John 8:56.)

Thus, the Passover Lamb was slain at Passover time on the north of the Altar of Moriah as an atonement for sin, which was the symbolic and typical purpose of all the lambs slain on the Temple altar

149

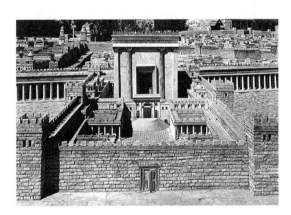

*Top left:* Antonia Fortress, as seen in the model city of New Testament Jerusalem at the Holyland Hotel, Jerusalem. *Top right:* "Skull Hill," possible site for Golgotha where Jesus was crucified. Some see the semblance of a face in the hillside. *Center left:* First-century burial tomb in the Shephelah, with a large stone to seal the entrance. This tomb would be similar to the tomb owned by Joseph of Arimathaea in Jerusalem. *Center right:* The southwest corner of the Temple Mount's retaining wall, which some consider the "pinnacle of the temple." (Matt. 4:5.) *Bottom left:* The Temple and its courts, as seen in the model city. The Court of the Gentiles is the great outer court, the Court of the Women is the enclosed area between the two gates, and the Court of the Priests is the area immediately around the Temple (center building). *Bottom right:* The altar of sacrifice in the Court of the Priests, as depicted in the model city.

over the centuries—those sacrifices all prefigured that greatest sacrifice.

### *"In this place is one greater than the temple." (Matt. 12:6.)*

No single place in all the world was holier to Jews and to Christians at the time of Jesus than the Temple Mount. It was known as *Har Habayit,* the "Mountain of the House [of God]." To this most sacred parcel of ground, the God of all creation could come to dwell and converse with his servants, the prophets and priests.

There is evidence in word and deed that Jesus considered the Temple to be the legitimate sanctuary of the true God. At one point he called it "my Father's house" (John 14:2); later he called it "my house" (Matt. 21:13). His life from beginning to end was bound up with the Temple. When his mother, Mary, had fulfilled the forty-day ritual of purification after giving birth, he was taken to the Temple in Jerusalem for the ceremonial redemption of the first-born. (See Luke 2:22–24.) At age twelve, he was found "in the temple, sitting in the midst of the doctors, both hearing them, and asking them questions." (Luke 2:46.)

Near the commencement of his ministry, "Jesus was taken up into the holy city, and the Spirit setteth him on the pinnacle of the temple" (JST, Matt. 4:5), where Satan tempted him. Along the whole length of the Temple Mount retaining walls, the southeast corner is the highest point—211 feet, or 64 meters. The distance, however, from the top of Herod's portico to the bottom of the Kidron was over four hundred feet! It is the traditional "pinnacle of the temple" to which Jesus

was brought.

Some researchers consider the southwestern corner of the Mount to be a more logical location for the temptation of Jesus because that corner has a much better angle for looking out over the city and because a specially carved platform stone was discovered in the toppled ruins of that corner. The stone indicated by a Hebrew inscription where a herald would blow the shofar, or ram's horn trumpet, to signal the advent of holy days. The traditional southeastern corner may be the more probable site, however, since it is the highest man-made height ever achieved anciently in the Holy Land, and the point of Satan's temptation was to entice Jesus into misusing his divine power by throwing himself off the dizzying height and counting on angels to rescue him from the fall. (See Matt. 4:6.)

The Gospels contain frequent notices of Jesus' activity in the Temple courts and in the Temple itself when he was in Jerusalem during his three-year ministry. Jesus declared of himself, "I spake openly to the world; I ever taught in the synagogue, and in the temple, whither the Jews always resort; and in secret have I said nothing." (John 18:20.)

Other references include the following: "The blind and the lame came to him in the temple; and he healed them." (Matt. 21:14.) "Now about the midst of the feast Jesus went up into the temple, and taught." (John 7:14.) "Early in the morning he came again into the temple, and all the people came unto him; and he sat down, and taught them." (John 8:2.) "He taught daily in the temple." (Luke 19:47.)

151

"All the people came early in the morning to him in the temple, for to hear him." (Luke 21:38.)

We have seen how Jesus routinely adapted into his teaching things from his immediate environs, often referring to something appropriate to the place where he taught. On one occasion, when in the Jerusalem Temple, he made figurative use of the Temple also. Hebrew literati for ages had used the Temple as a metaphor representing one's own body. "Jesus answered and said unto them, Destroy this temple, and in three days I will raise it up. Then said the Jews, Forty and six years was this temple in building, and wilt thou rear it up in three days? But he spake of the temple of his body." (John 2:19–21.)

According to the testimony of John, all this was said near the beginning of Jesus' ministry, which would make this declaration the first recorded foreshadowing of his death and resurrection. Evidently the Jews understood well his figurative language, that he referred not to Herod's forty-six-year temple building project, but to his own body, which he claimed power to raise up again after its death. At his hearing before the chief priests, one of the false witnesses testified, "This fellow said, I am able to destroy the temple of God, and to build it in three days." (Matt. 26:61.) At the cross, "they that passed by reviled him, wagging their heads, and saying, Thou that destroyest the temple, and buildest it in three days, save thyself." (Matt. 27:39–40.)

Through all of this, the Jewish leaders understood well Jesus' figure of speech. The following report is preserved of a con-versation after Jesus' death: "Now the next day, that followed the day of the preparation, the chief priests and Pharisees came together unto Pilate, saying, Sir, we remember that that deceiver said, while he was yet alive, *After three days I will rise again.* Command therefore that the sepulchre be made sure until the third day." (Matt. 27:62–64; italics added.)

The same symbolic use of the Temple appears in later New Testament writings. To the Christians in Corinth, a place where temples and temple prostitution were notorious, Paul wrote: "Know ye not that ye are the temple of God, and that the Spirit of God dwelleth in you? If any man defile the temple of God, him shall God destroy; for the temple of God is holy, which temple ye are." (1 Cor. 3:16–17.)

## The Temple at the Time of Jesus

The Temple of Herod was constructed with the help of ten thousand workmen. One thousand priests who had trained as masons helped to build the holiest parts, and a thousand wagons transported materials. The courtyards and porticoes were eight years under construction, and the Temple proper a year and a half. It was said that whoever had not seen the Temple of Herod had never seen a beautiful building. No other temple complex in the Graeco-Roman world compared with it in expansiveness and magnificence.

Although the architectural glories of Herod's Temple far surpassed Solomon's Temple, Herod's Temple had little of the former hallowed and spiritual atmosphere. The ark of the covenant, mercy

152

seat and cherubim, the Urim and Thummim providing revelatory contact with God, and other holy objects were lacking; and the Shechinah, the Divine Presence, was absent. And yet it was a place of revelation, as seen in the story of Zacharias (see Luke 1), and Jesus still acknowledged it as the Father's and his house.

Herod had nearly doubled the size of the Temple Mount from what it was during the period of the First Temple, making it in Jesus' day approximately forty acres in area. To expand so much, he had to extend the platform of the mount, particularly to the north, to the west, and to the south. To the north and west below floor level was earthfill, but to the south he supported the floor with vaults—rows of arched colonnades. The area under the floor of the southeast portion of the Temple courtyard, then, was hollow. There is now a large, columned chamber erroneously called "Solomon's Stables." Since it was constructed by Herod, the place did not exist in Solomon's day, though it was later used by the Crusaders for stabling horses.

The Temple Mount was a huge space measuring more than 132,000 square meters. The famous forum in Rome was only half that size, and the largest temple complex in the world—Karnak, in Upper Egypt, which was two thousand years in the building—is only a third bigger. Above ground on all sides of the Mount were extraordinary colonnaded porticoes (also called cloisters, that is, covered walkways with colonnades opening to the inside). Each portico hosted a double row of Corinthian columns, each column a monolith:

cut from one block of stone, each rose to over thirty-seven feet high. According to Josephus, Herod was responsible for extending the Mount northward, westward, and southward and erecting porticoes inside his newly positioned walls, but the eastern portico was built up by Herod in the same position as the previous Temple Mount.

This eastern portico was called Solomon's Porch. (See 1 Kgs. 6:3.) There Jesus, having come to the Passover at age twelve, conversed with the learned rabbis (see Luke 2:41–46); there he later walked and taught at the Feast of Dedication (Hanukkah) and testified that he was God's Son; and there the Jews tried to stone him (see John 10:22–39). Also Peter and John, after performing a miracle at the gate of the Temple, drew a large crowd in Solomon's Porch, preaching and calling for repentance following the denying and killing of the Holy One. And there they were arrested by Temple police and Sanhedrin officials. (See Acts 3:1–4:2.)

The southern portico, grander than the others, is often called Herod's Basilica. The word *basilica* (from the Greek *basileus*, meaning king and therefore designating a royal portico) meant a public hall that was rectangular in shape and had colonnaded aisles (a similar ground plan was adopted for early Christian churches). The Royal Basilica, or Portico, contained a total of 162 Corinthian columns. At its foot were the ramps leading onto the Temple courtyard from the south.

The eastern gate of the Temple Mount was called the Susa Gate. It faced eastward toward Susa (Shushan in the Bible), which

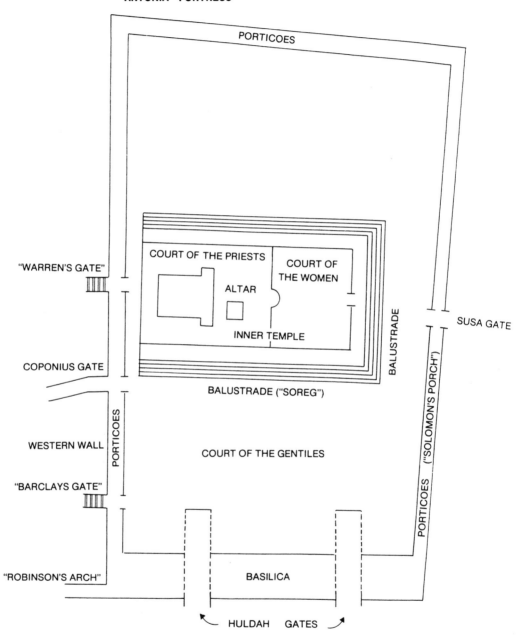

**ANTONIA FORTRESS**

PORTICOES

"WARREN'S GATE"

COURT OF THE PRIESTS

COURT OF THE WOMEN

ALTAR

INNER TEMPLE

BALUSTRADE

SUSA GATE

COPONIUS GATE

BALUSTRADE ("SOREG")

PORTICOES

WESTERN WALL

COURT OF THE GENTILES

PORTICOES ("SOLOMON'S PORCH")

"BARCLAYS GATE"

"ROBINSON'S ARCH"

BASILICA

HULDAH GATES

Map 6
The Temple Mount.

was the Persian capital where the biblical stories of Daniel, Esther, Nehemiah, and others in part unfolded. (See Dan. 8:2; Esth. 1:2; Neh. 1:1.) This gate was said to have been lower than the other gates so that the priests gathered across the bridge on the Mount of Olives for the sacrifice of the red heifer might still look directly into the Temple.

## Courts of the Temple

The outer court was called the Court of the Gentiles, where Jesus cast out the moneychangers. Non-Jews were allowed to enter this far onto the Temple Mount. Surrounding the Temple proper was a balustrade (Hebrew, *soreg*), an elevated stone railing about four and a half feet high with posted inscriptions in Greek and Latin warning gentiles not to pass beyond. One of these inscriptions was found in 1935 just outside the Lion's Gate of the Old City and is now on display in the Rockefeller Archaeological Museum. It reads: "No Gentile shall enter inward of the partition and barrier surrounding the Temple, and whosoever is caught shall be responsible to himself for his subsequent death." Roman authorities conceded to the Jewish religious leaders control of the sacred inner area to the point of capital punishment for non-Jews who passed beyond the stone railing.

A fortified inner wall with towers and gates surrounded the Court of the Women, which Israelite women were permitted to enter. The main gate into the Court of the Women was called the *Beautiful Gate* because of its rich decoration. At this gate Peter and John, on their way to Temple worship, stopped to hear the petition of a lame man. Peter dramatically healed the man, who joined them into the Temple, "walking, and leaping, and praising God." (Acts 3:1–11.)

The Court of the Women was a large space, nearly two hundred feet square. In the four corners were chambers for various functions. The eastern chambers served the Nazarites, where those who had made special vows could prepare their sacrifices, and another chamber was used for storing wood. The western chambers were used for storage of olive oil and for purification of lepers, which required a private ritual bath. It was perhaps to this Court of the Women that Joseph and Mary brought the infant Jesus five to six weeks (forty days) after birth in order for him as a firstborn to be redeemed and for Mary to be ceremonially cleansed. (See Luke 2:22–23.)

This whole court was surrounded by porticoes. Against the walls inside the porticoes were chests for charitable contributions, likely the place called "the treasury," where the widow cast in her mites (Mark 12:41–44) and where Jesus taught during the Feast of Tabernacles (see John 8:20). There Jesus bore witness of his own divinity, dealt mercifully with the woman taken in adultery, proclaimed himself the Light of the World and the Messiah, and bore testimony that he was the God of Abraham. Jews tried to stone him again. (See John 7–8.)

Fifteen curved steps and then the Gate of Nicanor led into the innermost court. (Nicanor was a wealthy Jew from Alexandria who donated the ornate doors of

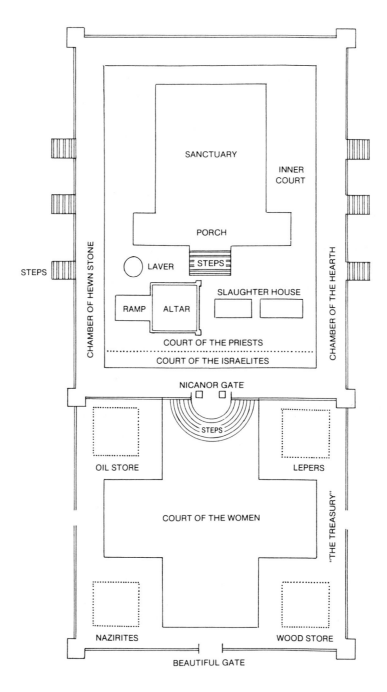

Map 7
The Inner Temple.

the gate.) Only priests and other authorized Temple officiators would enter this court. To the sides of its porticoes were the Chamber of the Hearth, where priests on duty could spend their nights, and the Chamber of Hewn Stone, where the Sanhedrin met. In the latter chamber, before the council, Stephen was transfigured (see Acts 6:12–15) and later Paul testified (see Acts 22:30–23:10).

On the north side of this court, which was actually a double court (first the Court of the Men of Israel, then the Priests' Court), was the Place of Slaughtering. On the south side was the giant brass wash basin, or laver, supported on the backs of twelve lions. For all the water needs of the Temple Mount, millions of gallons of water were brought in from Solomon's Pools, south of Bethlehem, and stored in a connected series of rock-cut reservoirs, or cisterns.

Near the laver, the great horned altar of sacrifice or burnt offering stood, measuring forty-eight feet square and fifteen feet high! Some think that the huge rock mass inside the Dome of the Rock — which now measures approximately forty × fifty × seven feet high — once formed the base of the altar of sacrifice. At least it is clear from scripture that King David purchased the rock in order to build an altar to the Lord. (See 2 Sam. 24:18–25.) The altar consisted of whitewashed unhewn stone, and it had a ramp leading up to it from the south that was forty-eight feet long and twenty-four feet wide.

The altar stood off center in the court so that the priest sacrificing the red heifer (a symbolic representation of the Savior)

could see straight into the giant entryway of the Holy Sanctuary, which stood sixty-six feet high and thirty-three feet wide (twenty × ten meters). The Sanctuary, or Holy Place, was made of marble. Two columns in front were named Jachin and Boaz (meaning "He will establish" and "In him is strength"), after the names of the entry columns of Solomon's Temple. The Temple proper was over one hundred fifty feet high (today's Dome of the Rock reaches a height of just over one hundred feet) and was surrounded on top by golden spikes to discourage birds from landing on and tarnishing the stone.

Inside the Holy Place was the veil leading to the most sacred chamber, the Holy of Holies. That same veil was torn from top to bottom at the death of Jesus. (See Matt. 27:51.) Whereas only the high priest once a year could enter the symbolic presence of God, now Jesus, through his death, rent that partition, signifying the availability of all people to reach God's presence. (See Heb. 9:11–14; 10:19–22 for Paul's explanation of the symbolism.) The rending of the Temple veil may also denote the rending of the Judaism of the Mosaic dispensation.

Overall, the Temple area consisted of a series of rising platforms. From the Court of the Gentiles, one ascended stairs to the Court of the Women; from there, one ascended the fifteen curved stairs (possibly singing fifteen Psalms of Ascent, Ps. 120–34) to the Court of the Men of Israel and the Court of the Priests; and finally an ascent was requisite to enter the Holy Place itself. Thus a phrase like "Jesus went up into the temple" (John 7:14) is quite literal.

One of the Psalms of Ascent says, "I was glad when they said unto me, Let us go into the house of the Lord. Our feet shall stand within thy gates, O Jerusalem. Jerusalem is builded as a city that is compact together: whither the tribes go up, the tribes of the Lord, unto the testimony of Israel, to give thanks unto the name of the Lord. . . . Pray for the peace of Jerusalem: they shall prosper that love thee. . . . Because of the house of the Lord our God I will seek thy good." (Ps. 122:1–4, 6, 9.)

# SCRIPTURE INDEX

161

21:39, p. 50
22:3, p. 50
22:6, p. 62
22:24, p. 145
22:30–23:10, p. 157
23:10, p. 145
23:23, p. 40
23:31, p. 40
23:34, p. 50
23:35, p. 145
24–26, p. 40
24:18, p. 50
24:26, p. 130
25:1, p. 5
25:23, p. 13
26:13, pp. 12, 62
26:20, pp. 17, 21
27:2, p. 133
27:3, p. 48
27:6, p. 133
28:11, p. 133

**Romans**

1:13, p. 82
7:4, p. 82
8:36, p. 108
9:27, p. 69
9:33, p. 68
11:16, p. 78
11:17, pp. 85, 97
11:24, p. 97
14:2, p. 90

**1 Corinthians**

3:6–9, p. 78
3:16–17, p. 152
5:6–8, p. 84
5:7, p. 108
9:7, p. 105
9:9, p. 111

**2 Corinthians**

3:3, p. 67
4:7, p. 69
6:14, p. 111
9:6, p. 77
11:3, p. 124
12:7, p. 103

**Galatians**

4:24–25, p. 38
5:1, p. 111
5:22, p. 82

6:7, p. 77
6:8, p. 77
6:9, p. 79

**Ephesians**

2:20, p. 68

**Philippians**

1:11, p. 82
1:22, p, 82
3:2, p. 127

**1 Timothy**

5:18, p. 111
6:10, p. 130

**2 Timothy**

2:6, p. 93
2:20, p. 69

**Titus**

3:14, p. 82

**Hebrews**

6:8, p. 103
7:14, p. 20
8:5, p. 38
9, p. 109
9–10, p. 93
9:11–14, p. 157
9:19–20, p. 91
9:19, p. 126
10:4, p. 109
10:19–22, p. 157
11:12, pp. 8, 69
11:17, p. 149
11:29, p. 38
11:37, p. 105
11:38, p. 8
12:11, p. 82
13:15, p. 82
13:20, p. 107

**James**

1:10–11, p. 101
1:11, p. 58
3:4, p. 60
3:8, p. 122
3:11–12, p. 55
3:11, p. 53
4:8, p. 53
5:1–5, p. 130
5:2, p. 124

5:3, pp. 72–73
5:7, pp. 79, 93
5:14, p. 86
5:17–18, p. 59

**1 Peter**

1:7, p. 73
1:18, p. 73
1:24–25, p. 101
1:24, pp. 77, 101
2:6, p. 68
2:7–8, p. 68
2:25, p. 107
3:20–21, p. 52
5:2–3, p. 108
5:4, p. 107

**2 Peter**

1:12, p. 55
2:6, pp. 14, 38
2:17, p. 55
2:22, p. 127

**1 John**

1:29, p. 108
1:36, p. 108
5:2, p. 140

**Jude**

1:7, p. 38
1:14, p. 81

**Revelations**

1:14, p. 63
2:7, p. 97
2:27, pp. 71, 73
3:18, p. 73
5:8, p. 108
5:12, p. 108
6:6, p. 132
6:16, p. 108
7:14, p. 108
9:3, p. 125
9:5, p. 124
9:7, p. 124
9:9, p. 73
9:10, p. 124
9:20, p. 73
11:1, p. 103
12:5, p. 73
12:9, p. 124
13:8, p. 108
14:15, p. 79

14:18, p. 93
14:20, p. 93
15:6, p. 89
17:3, p. 126
17:4, p. 126
17:14, p. 108
18:12, pp. 69, 73, 126
18:13, p. 134
18:16, p. 126
18:17, p. 132
19:7, p. 108
19:9, p. 108
19:15, pp. 73, 93
19:20, p. 71
20:2, p. 124
21:2–4, pp. 135, 137
21:8, p. 71
21:9, p. 108
21:15–16, p. 103
21:18, p. 73
21:21, pp. 73, 134
21:22–24, pp. 135, 137
21:23, p. 108
21:27, p. 108

**BOOK OF MORMON**

**1 Nephi**

10:9, p. 37

**2 Nephi**

25:5–6, p. 1

**Alma**

33:19–20, p. 122

**Helaman**

8:13–15, p. 122

**DOCTRINE AND COVENANTS**

18:1–7, p. 83
86:2–3, pp. 83–84
86:7, p. 84

**PEARL OF GREAT PRICE**

**Moses**

6:63, p. 2

# INDEX

Boldface numbers indicate pages with maps or photographs.

D. Kelly Ogden is associate professor of ancient scripture at Brigham Young University and has taught courses in Hebrew, the Old and New Testament, the Bible as literature, history of the ancient Near East, and biblical and modern geography of the Holy Land. For a span of fourteen years, he helped administer BYU's study programs in the Holy Land and guided students on field study trips all over Israel, the Sinai, Egypt, Jordan, Turkey, and Greece. He led groups of students on many "walks" through the Holy Land, including retracing the "three-day's journey" (fifty-three miles) of Abraham and Isaac from Beersheba to Mount Moriah, the ninety-two miles Joseph and Mary traveled from Nazareth to Bethlehem, the two hundred miles from Dan to Beersheba, and the two-hundred mile "Lehi trek" from Jerusalem to the Red Sea.

Dr. Ogden received a B.A. in English and Spanish from Weber State College, Ogden, Utah; an M.Ed. in international education from Brigham Young University, Provo, Utah; an M.A. in Hebrew language and historical geography of the Bible from the Institute of Holy Land Studies, Jerusalem, Israel; and a Ph.D. in Middle East studies from the University of Utah, Salt Lake City, Utah.

He is the author of several books on the Holy Land, including *Historical Geography in the Bible* (Jerusalem and Provo: The Jerusalem Center for Near Eastern Studies, in conjunction with Pictorial Archive, 1988) and *The Holy Land — a Geographical, Historical, and Archaeological Guide to the Land of the Bible,* co-authored with Jeffrey R. Chadwick (Jerusalem: Barry Segal International, 1990). Several of his articles on the scriptures have appeared in the *Ensign,* the *Studies in Scriptures* series, and *Encyclopedia of Mormonism.*